SEARCHING

...IT'S NOT WHAT. IT'S WHO.

To order additional copies of *Searching . . .* ,
by Omar Miranda, **call 1-800-765-6955.**

Visit us at **www.reviewandherald.com** for information
on other Review and Herald® products.

SEARCHING

...IT'S NOT WHAT. IT'S WHO.

OMAR MIRANDA

An Ex-Addict Talks Straight About the Importance of Knowing, Loving, and Living Jesus

REVIEW AND HERALD® PUBLISHING ASSOCIATION
Since 1861 | www.reviewandherald.com

The Review and Herald® Publishing Association publishes biblically based materials for spiritual, physical, and mental growth and Christian discipleship.

Review and Herald® books may be purchased in bulk for educational, business, fund-raising, or sales promotional use. For information, e-mail specialmarkets@reviewandherald.com.

This book was
Edited by Lori Peckham
Cover design by Daniel Anez / Review and Herald® Design Center
Cover illustration © BibleGallery.com / Jack Pardue
Interior design by Emily Ford / Review and Herald® Design Center
Typeset Minion Pro 11/13

Library of Congress Control Number: 2014930261

ISBN 978-0-8280-2752-6

DEDICATION

First, I'd like to dedicate this book to my Lord and Savior, Jesus Christ, who by His incredible and indescribable power and love died on the cross to save me—and then He never stopped calling me, and eventually wooed me back to Him . . . even after I kicked Him to the curb so many times.

Second, this book is dedicated to my parents, who made sure that we had worship twice a day. (Yes, Papi, I too have to get on my son about coming to worship without a shirt on!) Mami and Papi, thanks for your daily faithfulness in reading your Bible, reading Christian books, and praying. Even more so, thanks for being joyful in your Christian life, as well as being honest and real about your ups and downs with your relationship with Jesus. Thanks for involving us kids in *every* church activity, and thank you, thank you, thank you for *never* stopping loving me and praying for me . . . even in the midst of my rebellion, sin, anger, and addictions.

Third, I'd like to dedicate this book to my wife, Renee, and my two children, Isabella and Jackson. Renee, thanks for your unswerving faith and belief in the fact that God could redeem my "crazy" and bring something great out of it. I love you so much. Without your prayers, love, patience, encouragement, and support, I wouldn't have been able to complete this monumental project. Isabella and Jacko, the initial impetus of this book—and all of my writing—has come out of my love for you both. I hope you learn from Daddy's mistakes so you don't have to make the same ones. Thanks for teaching me about the love, grace, mercy, compassion, and patience of God.

Fourth, I want to dedicate this book to Mr. Bass, a boys' dean and Bible teacher extraordinaire. He is a godly man, husband, and father, as well as my mentor and friend. Mr. Bass, thanks for your nightly chapel worships in which you challenged us to draw closer to Jesus. More important, thanks for daily living out what you believed. You've made an eternal difference in my life.

"Young people brought up in an Adventist home often understand being a Christian as believing the doctrines of the church and obeying Christian standards. In *Searching* . . . Omar Miranda refocuses the attention to the central requirement of having a relationship with Jesus. This is primary—everything else follows. Every teenager should be encouraged to read this book."

—**Roger Dudley,** Emeritus Professor of Christian Ministry; Emeritus Director, Institute of Church Ministry, Andrews University; Author

"Join the search! Author Omar Miranda takes you through his own journey, which will have many touchpoints with your own. He moves past the easy answers and wrestles with the messiness of life for the person who wants to live for Christ."

—**Steve Case,** President, Involve Youth; Coordinator, Youth and Young Adult Ministry at the Doctor of Ministry program at the Seventh-day Adventist Theological Seminary at Andrews University; Author

"Jesus is the first word and the last word. He is the word on the street and the word in our souls, an always-present help in patches of plenty and times of trouble. In *Searching* . . . Omar brings the Word to life, breaking down and lifting up what this forever friendship with Jesus means and brings."

—**Chris Blake,** Former Editor, *Insight* magazine; Professor of English and Communication, Union College; Author

"Get your highlighter out when you read this book! It's full of highlights for living the Christian life, and you will want to review them again and again."

—**Mike Jones,** Former Editor, *Insight* magazine; Author

"The force behind the popular Miranda Writes advice column once again demonstrates his uncanny knack for helping teens not merely to survive but actually to thrive as they make their way toward adulthood. Omar digs deeply into his counseling past and produces a gold mine of godly wisdom and practical help for facing a vast range of challenging personal and social issues. And he does it all with grace and candor, pointing readers to the ultimate Source of hope, Jesus Christ."

—**Randy Fishell,** Editor, *Guide and Real* magazines

ACKNOWLEDGMENTS

I would like to thank all the patient and hardworking people at the Review and Herald Publishing Association. Specifically, I want to thank the recent past *Insight* editor and present vice president for editorial services, Dwain Esmond, and recent past *Insight* assistant editor, Tom Fraga.

Dwain, thanks for having that initial conversation with me several years ago, and thanks for your faith in my vision and for the courage to make it happen. You are truly one of "the sons of Isaachar, who had understanding of the times" (see 1 Chronicles 12:32). I hope that together we will continue to be able to love, serve, and lead teens into the strong, sure arms of Jesus.

Tom, thanks for being "Mr. Consistent" (aka the "bad cop") and speaking the truth in love. Many days you repeated your mantra: "Too long, Omar; trim the fat!" It's because of you that I'm a better writer. You made me look good—and that's hard to do.

"I have found Omar Miranda's *Searching* . . . inspiring because it turns us to the Bible. Like Ellen White, Omar encourages the reader to find answers and wisdom in God's Word. His material is Bible-based, and he talks about action change as well as thought change. So much that is written on these topics talks only about an attitude change, but as a 'doer,' I really appreciate how Omar talks about actions that will reinforce and demonstrate attitude change."

—**Lori Peckham,** Former Editor, *Insight* magazine

"In this book Omar Miranda helps you not to fall for the devil and the world's lies. Not only does this book unmask the devil—it also equips you with Bible verses and examples to help you combat the enemy as he tries to deceive you. Omar helps you realize that nothing or nobody in this world can ever fill that hole in your heart that your soul desperately hungers for. Nobody, that is, but Jesus."

—**Willy Ramos,** Lay Pastor, Lighthouse Community Church

Searching . . . is the book that every young person is searching for. Omar uses his past experiences to connect with them on a real down-to-earth level, while showing them how to find what they are truly searching for—Jesus. Each chapter will show them how to reach out and connect with Jesus in a practical and powerful way. Get this book in the hand of every young person you know!

—**Jeremy J. Anderson,** Youth/Young Adult Motivational Speaker; Author

"Miranda addresses the nuts and bolts of a relationship with Jesus in a realistic and thought-provoking manner."

—**Glen Robinson,** Professor of Communication,
Southwestern Adventist University

"Omar is a man with a passion! He has a passion for his Lord and Savior. And he has a passion to share the message of salvation with young people. As a counselor he has counseled with hundreds of young people and has a rare insight to the struggles our young people face today. As I read through this book I felt as though I was reading a modern young person's version of one of my favorite books, *Steps to Christ*. Within each chapter you will discover the love of Jesus shining through. His everyday stories keep your attention, and he makes the message of salvation so simple to understand and accept. I am confident you will experience Jesus and gain a deeper understanding of His love for you as you delve into the pages of *Searching* . . . "

—**Bill Bass,** Bible Teacher, Fletcher Academy

"The Christian says, 'Creatures are not born with desires unless satisfaction for those desires exists. A baby feels hunger: well, there is such a thing as food. A duckling wants to swim: well, there is such a thing as water. Men feel sexual desire: well, there is such a thing as sex. If I find in myself a desire which no experience in this world can satisfy, the most probable explanation is that I was made for another world. If none of my earthly pleasures satisfy it, that does not prove that the universe is a fraud. Probably earthly pleasures were never meant to satisfy it, but only to arouse it, to suggest the real thing. If that is so, I must take care, on the one hand, never to despise, or to be unthankful for, these earthly blessings, and on the other, never to mistake them for the something else of which they are only a kind of copy, or echo, or mirage. I must keep alive in myself the desire for my true country, which I shall not find till after death; I must never let it get snowed under or turned aside; I must make it the main object of life to press on to that country and to help others to do the same."

—C. S. Lewis, Mere Christianity

"Suppose someone should offer me a plateful of crumbs after I had eaten a T-bone steak. I would say, 'No, thank you. I am already satisfied.' Christian, that is the secret—you can be so filled with the things of Christ, so enamored with the things of God, that you do not have time for the sinful pleasures of the world."

—Billy Graham

TABLE OF CONTENTS

Introduction....13
Hole in Our Soul....19
My *New* New Year's Resolutions....20
Dead Man Walking....21
Simple?....23
Is Your Jesus Used Up and Broken Down?....26
Merry Christmas . . . I Cleaned Up Your Mess!....28
"You're Not My Daddy!"....29
There's Nothing You Can Do to Make Me Stop Loving You....33
The Cosmic Conflict....34
Life's Curveballs....36
Who You Are and Whose You Are....38
Dirty Diapers and Difficult Daily Decisions....40
Say "Uncle!"....42
God Wants Us to Eat Meat....46
Spiritual Physical....49
Rotten Fruit Means Rotten Root....61
Modern Warfare: God's Style....65
Great Is Thy Faithfulness!....71
The Squeaky Wheel Gets the Grease....72
Be God's Balloon....75
I Like the Smell of Clean....76
You're Dirty!....78
Light's Out?....79
It's Raining Cats and Dogs!....84

The Problem of Pain 87
Big Brother Is Watching 89
The Gridiron of Life 91
Be a Cookie-cutter Christian 94
Disney World Death 96
Closed-minded Christian 98
Why Are You a Firework? 101
What to Do When God Asks You to Give Up Your Dream 103
Stop, Drop, and Roll! 109
What to Do When You're Not Sure How to Share Your Faith 112
Worldview Wars 117
Unapologetic About Apologetics 122
Lit Up: Glowing for Jesus 128
How Not to Be a Fool (Living Life Wisely) 132
Your Replacement Is Here! 141
Is There Anyone Like Me Out There? 143
The Secret to Contentment 146
Stinking Thinking 151
What's on Your Key Chain? 155
Five Conclusions 157

INTRODUCTION

You're hungry . . . I know you're hungry! You're hungry for something to fill the collective holes in your soul that are within all of us. I've come to the realization that every unhealthy thing we do to try to fill the God-shaped hole in our soul is a search . . . It's all a search for God. King Solomon, known as the richest and wisest man who has ever lived, spent almost his entire lifetime searching for something . . . anything . . . that would give him that deep sense of fulfillment. He finally found it in one place: a relationship with God, respecting Him and doing life His way. Of course, this was after wasting much of his life and emotionally, spiritually, and physically injuring himself.

To my horror, I've seen—and continue to see—many of you doing the same thing. You're wasting your time spinning your spiritual, sexual, relational, and emotional wheels looking all over this world for the connection, significance, meaning, purpose, joy, peace, and power that only living a life with and in Jesus can give you. In the process you're getting yourselves involved in all kinds of crazy sins, leading to unhealthy and dysfunctional habits, relationships, lifestyles, diseases, and addictions. Ultimately you're unable to be the best that you can be for yourselves, for God, and for others. So instead of offering your bodies up to God as living sacrifices so you can test God's pleasing and perfect will (see Romans 12:1, 2), you end up offering your bodies up to sin, the world, and ultimately the devil. What a waste!

You need Jesus today more than any other time in this world's history! First, you need to find and *keep* a daily, real, and honest relationship with Jesus. You have to understand that He is first your Savior to make you free and then your Lord to *keep* you free! Additionally, that relationship needs to positively transform how you live, love, and connect with others—in all kinds of relationships.

You need connection! You need to connect with parents, teachers, youth pastors, youth leaders, and other caring adults who are not only unconditionally loving toward you, but also striving to live a godly, joyous Christian life. And they need to be honest with you about their own life experiences—past and present, positive and negative.

Many of you are hurting. Over the years I've seen the results of what Chap Clark in his shocking book *Hurt: Inside the World of Today's Teenagers* rightly terms "systemic abandonment": the near-total, purposeful, multidimensional abandonment of you teens by every social and emotional support that is important to your overall healthy development.

WHY DID I WASTE MY TIME WRITING THIS BOOK?

Our relationship with God is central to who we are and what we do, think, and feel—about everything! If we get this first and most important relationship wrong, then everything else in our lives will be messed up as well.

I began writing this book for my two children. I wanted to break down this most difficult relationship for them. I wanted to put it in the simplest terms I could. Then I realized that somebody else had already done it. The apostle Paul, writing in one of his famous rants (I'm pretty sure he had ADD), boils down the message of this entire book to this: "Nothing is as wonderful as knowing Christ Jesus my Lord. I have given up everything else and count it all as garbage. All I want is Christ and to know that I belong to him. . . . All I want is to know Christ and the power that raised him to life" (Philippians 3:8-10).

Everything else that happens to us in our lives is contingent upon our correct recognition that we are made for a relationship with Jesus. This book is about working on cultivating that as the "root" of our lives. It's about being proactive; unfortunately, there are a lot of "fruit" behaviors (depression, anxiety, addiction, cutting, sex before marriage, porn, etc.) that come out of our sincere search for our "root." This is our "Solomon search."

With that being said, I want to welcome you to what I hope is the beginning of the *end* of your search. I, with Paul, want to tell you the glorious and incredible news: "God's plan was to make me a servant of his church and to send me to preach his complete message to you. For ages and ages this message was kept secret from everyone, but now it has been explained to God's people. God did this because he wanted you . . .

to understand his wonderful and glorious mystery. And the mystery is that Christ lives in you, and he is your hope of sharing in God's glory. We announce the message about Christ, and we use all our wisdom to warn and teach everyone, so that all of Christ's followers will grow and become mature. That's why I work so hard and use the mighty power he gives me" (Colossians 1:25-29).

I want to introduce you to Jesus so you can see for yourself the joy, peace, significance, belonging, and power of having a real relationship with Him. Why is this important? Because when Jesus comes back, the only way you'll be invited to the party of a lifetime—for eternity—is to know Him . . . not know about Him or even do a lot of stuff for Him. It's about who you know, plain and simple. Jesus said it best; let's take a look at it. It was right at the end of Jesus' sermon on the mount, the longest recorded block of Jesus talking. Jesus had basically laid out the foundation of His ministry—how someone who is focused on God's kingdom will talk, think, and act.

" 'Enter through the narrow gate. For wide is the gate and broad is the road that leads to destruction, and many enter through it. But small is the gate and narrow the road that leads to life, and only a few find it.

" 'Watch out for false prophets. They come to you in sheep's clothing, but inwardly they are ferocious wolves. By their fruit you will recognize them. Do people pick grapes from thornbushes, or figs from thistles? Likewise, every good tree bears good fruit, but a bad tree bears bad fruit. A good tree cannot bear bad fruit, and a bad tree cannot bear good fruit. Every tree that does not bear good fruit is cut down and thrown into the fire. Thus, by their fruit you will recognize them.

" 'Not everyone who says to me, "Lord, Lord," will enter the kingdom of heaven, but only the one who does the will of my Father who is in heaven. Many will say to me on that day, "Lord, Lord, did we not prophesy *in your name [Christians by name only]* and *in your name* drive out demons and *in your name* perform many miracles?" *[behaviors and actions—not taking into account emotions, motivations, and the heart]* Then I will tell them plainly, "I never knew you. Away from me, you evildoers!"

" 'Therefore everyone who hears these words of mine and puts them into practice is like a wise man who built his house on the rock. The rain came down, the streams rose, and the winds blew and beat against that house; yet it did not fall, because it had its foundation on the rock. But everyone who hears these words of mine and does not put them into practice is like a foolish man who built his house on sand. The rain came down, the streams rose, and the winds blew and beat against that house, and it fell with a great crash.'

"When Jesus had finished saying these things, the crowds were amazed at his teaching, because he taught as one who had authority, and not as their teachers of the law" (Matthew 7:13-29, NIV).

Let me summarize what He said, because it's the core reason I wrote this book.

It doesn't matter what you call yourself. Those whom Jesus knows are those who, at the core of their being, want to know Jesus more and more every day (Philippians 3:7-11)—and based on that relationship and love, they do good works.

Good works, devoid of a relationship with Jesus, will not be enough to get you into heaven.

There will be people who think that they know Jesus and that their good works are the best measure of their relationship with Him, but they will be sorely disappointed.

I want you to realize that trying to do life any other way than God's way won't work. When God says "Don't," what He's really saying is "Don't hurt yourself!" God loves you and recognizes that living life on this earth is hard enough without dealing with negative consequences brought about by our own bad choices.

In this book you'll read about what I wish I would have been taught as a child, teen, and college student, but I had to learn it all the hard way! I was raised in a strong Bible-believing, God-worshipping home in which my parents respected, honored, and obeyed God, but I didn't see the same example in my church. What I saw was predominantly a Bible-believing, doctrine-teaching, *hard* church. I saw a lot of hypocritical, critical, miserable, mean people. There was a lot of truth, but not a lot of love. There were lots of judgment and condemnation and little to no joy, love, understanding, grace, discernment, and kindness.

WHAT'S THIS BOOK ABOUT?

This book is a compilation of Miranda Writes, my column for *Insight* magazine (insightmagazine.org), which were my general rants, ravings, and ponderings about what I've learned in life with—and without—Jesus. It's all basically about how to better know Jesus, love Jesus, and live Jesus!

You're probably asking yourself, "Why did he choose to write about this?" Because if you don't get this whole getting-to-know-Jesus thing right, then *nothing else matters*! I've seen this in my own life and in the lives of a lot of young people: If you don't get this one thing right, it could seriously mess up your life and others' lives really quickly for a really long time. I'm not going to apologize for my boldness and honesty. I'm tired of seeing you teens flushing all your awesomeness down the toilet of life because you're not finding what you're truly searching for!

WHY BOTHER TO READ THIS BOOK?

I think I've got a lot of commonsense stuff to say about living your life and dealing with your issues both with and apart from God. I'd like to think I deal with issues in a humorous, honest, but always biblical way. I'm hoping to give you information not just about how to live your life, but about how to life your live *God's way*. I've got lots of unique experiences in four different areas:

EX-ADDICT: This is the one that I think qualifies me the most to talk to you about issues, because for about 15 years of my life I went off the deep end. As I said before, I was raised in the church, but turned my back on my family, my church, and my God. I lost my mind and made some really stupid decisions in my life that I'm not proud of. I was a really angry guy. I'm a recovering sex and porn addict. The truth is, I'm still feeling the consequences of some of those bad habits, sins, and addictions to this day.

COUNSELOR: I've been dealing with teens and their families for more than 20 years, and I hear about the issues they're dealing with every day. I've also got a master's degree in counseling.

CHRISTIAN: I've been a Christian since I was about 8, so I have a lot of life experiences I can share with you. I feel that I've got a pretty strong relationship with God, but neither I nor my relationship with God is perfect. Every day I make choices that can drive me either closer to God or further from Him. I still say and do stupid stuff *every day*—just ask my wife and kids.

FATHER: It's absolutely amazing what happens to a person when they have children. It's like all of a sudden you really start to understand more deeply how God feels about you—how patient and loving He is toward you and your knuckleheadedness. I don't claim to be God, but I'm starting to see a lot of stuff from His point of view.

When you're done with this book, it's my greatest hope that you will:

- grow and flourish in your relationship with God, through Jesus
- not make stupid mistakes that get you tangled up in years and years

of chronic sin, addictions, bad life choices, and the consequences that go with them (instead, you'll be able to sidestep those things)
- share that love, belonging, fulfillment, power, and purpose that you've found in Christ with as many people as you can
- speed Christ's return so we can all go home to spend eternity with Jesus, God, and the Holy Spirit

I want to leave you with the last words of an older Christian to a younger Christian who was getting started in his relationship with God. He said this: "Don't let anyone make fun of you, just because you are young. Set an example for other followers by what you say and do, as well as by your love, faith, and purity" (1 Timothy 4:12). It's my hope that you will not only live a happy, healthy, productive, and fulfilled life, but also be a *positive* example for others by how you live.

I want to help you know Jesus, love Jesus, and live Jesus! God bless you as you move forward in God's power and strength to clear away anything that gets between you and God. When you find God, through Jesus, you'll find what you've been searching for all along!

I would love your feedback! Share your thoughts, questions, stories, and pictures at:

E-MAIL: omarmiranda@comcast.net
WEB: http://omirandawrites.wordpress.com
TWITTER: @MirandaWritesOn
FACEBOOK: Omar Miranda

HOLE IN OUR SOUL

It was like the running of the bulls in Spain!" My wife was describing a 5:00 a.m. sale at Walmart the day after Thanksgiving. She had arrived at 4:45 a.m., and the parking lot had been packed.

I responded in usual man fashion: "Why did you go? It's just stuff!" We live in a fake world. Like a chocolate Easter bunny, it's sweet at first but hollow, leaving us with a bad aftertaste and yearning for true satisfaction. But for what?

A story I read in November 2008 caught my eye. "Wal-Mart Death Preventable: Jdimytai Damour, 34, was crushed as he and other employees attempted to unlock the doors of a Long Island, New York, store at 5:00 a.m. Friday, police said. . . . A line began forming at 9:00 p.m. Thursday and . . . by 5:00 a.m. Friday, there were as many as 2,000 customers outside. A video showed about a dozen people knocked to the ground as the doors were opened and the crowd surged, breaking the doors. Minutes later, police trying to give Damour first aid were jostled by customers still running into the store."*

Is stuff that important? No, it's the *hole that the stuff is trying to fill* that's important. Each of us was created with a hole in our soul—an indescribable need for an intimate relationship with God that nothing can ever fill . . . except God Himself.

Solomon, the wisest man *ever*, spent almost his entire life searching for fulfillment and meaning. In his frustration—but to our benefit—he wrote down in his diary everything he learned, and we have it in the form of the biblical Old Testament book called Ecclesiastes.

What he ultimately learned is truly life-changing. Solomon starts his diary on a promising note, stating that everything in life is a waste of time (see Ecclesiastes 1:2). He goes on to write: "All of life is far more boring than words could ever say. Our eyes and our ears are never satisfied with what we see and hear. Everything that happens has happened before; nothing is new, nothing under the sun. Someone might say, 'Here is something new!' But it happened before, long before we were born" (Ecclesiastes 1:8-10).

Solomon rants and raves for 11 chapters. He writes that he literally had enough money to get anything he wanted. "I got whatever I wanted and did whatever made me happy. . . . Then I thought about everything I had done . . . and it was simply chasing the wind. Nothing on earth is worth the trouble" (Ecclesiastes 2:10, 11).

In the end Solomon admits that nothing brought him the happiness and fulfillment he was searching for. In chapter 12 he gives us his final conclusions. Here's the secret of life that the smartest person *ever* wasted almost his entire life looking for: "Fear God [revere and worship Him, knowing that He is] and keep His commandments, for this is the whole of man [the full, original purpose of his creation, the object of God's providence, the root of character, the foundation of all happiness, the adjustment to all inharmonious circumstances and conditions under the sun] *and* the whole [duty] for every man" (Ecclesiastes 12:13, Amplified).

So there you have it. The tale of one man's—actually, all humanity's—search for satisfaction, fulfillment, peace, and joy. Solomon said it straight: God's way isn't the only way, but it's the best way. I hope you won't waste any of your own life trying to live it apart from God. Take it from Sol—it's a waste of time.

---

*www.cnn.com/2008/US/11/29/black.friday.death/index.html

MY *NEW* NEW YEAR'S RESOLUTIONS

It's a new year, and it's time to think about resolutions. This year I'm keeping it simple. I'm focusing on relationships: loving God and loving people.

Jesus was all about keeping it simple. He didn't let anyone or anything get in the way of what He was on earth to do. Jesus expressed His job most clearly in a conversation He had with somebody who didn't like Him and was trying to trick Him into saying something that would get Him in trouble—possibly thrown in jail or even killed! But He spoke to the guy anyway, because that's what Jesus was all about: trying to build bridges—relationships—with people who were against Him.

Here's what happened. This guy asked Jesus what the most important commandment was: "Jesus answered: Love the Lord your God with all your heart, soul, and mind. This is the first and most important commandment. The second most important commandment is like this one. And it is, 'Love others as much as you love yourself.' All the Law of Moses and the Books of the Prophets are based on these two commandments" (Matthew 22:37-40).

The best thing that you and I can do—the thing that most pleases God and most clearly shows others what He's really about—is to love God supremely and to love everyone else as much as we love ourselves.

Let's unpack the meaning of what Jesus said. We need to give God all of our lives and not hold anything back. More important, by loving God with all we've got and all we are, we give Him permission to give us the motivation and the power through His Holy Spirit to not just love others, but love them *as much as we love ourselves.*

DEAD MAN WALKING

In the last chapter I introduced my *new* New Year's resolutions: (1) to love God with all my heart, soul, mind, and strength, and (2) to love others as I love myself. But that's easier said than done! In this chapter we'll discuss this struggle between good and evil in our own lives. We'll come to the realization that the fiercest war in the world is not being fought in Afghanistan, Iraq, or some other part of the world; it's being fought in our own minds and bodies—between ourselves, God, Satan, and the world

Before we can examine the "what" of loving God and others, we've got to examine the "how." How is it possible for me to actually be unselfish and truly love God and others with all I've got? I can't, and that's why I need God.

The Bible makes it really clear that we were all born sinful and evil. The Bible says: "Adam sinned, and that sin brought death into the world. Now everyone has sinned, and so everyone must die" (Romans 5:12). Thanks to Adam and Eve, everybody born after them has been dealing with this sin problem. Adam and Eve basically traded their perfect Garden of Eden home and their close, face-to-face relationship with God for a bite of fruit

(Genesis 2:15-17). So there's no hope for any of us? Not so. Jesus Christ already made it right for us!

The Bible says: "Christ died for us at a time when we were helpless and sinful" (Romans 5:6). But here's the coolest part: Jesus' perfect life, death, and return from the dead paid the price for our sin and "unmessed" the mess that Adam's sin brought (see Romans 5:17-21).

So it shouldn't be hard for you and me to love God and others with our whole being—but it *is* hard. So hard! I mean, if I've been saved by accepting the perfect life and death of Jesus as my substitute, why is it still so hard to love God and others unselfishly? Here's the bottom line: Jesus' sacrifice gave us the power to be freed from the results of sin (justification), but we still struggle with the power of sin (sanctification). We won't be done with sin totally until we get to heaven (glorification).

Sinners don't feel bad or get frustrated when they can't do right. But we Christians do get frustrated about that. There's a constant war going on inside of us. We struggle a lot with this issue, because we love Jesus and want to be like Him. The most difficult war we Christians face is the war going on inside of us between the sinful nature we were born with and the spiritual nature that the Holy Spirit provides when we accept Jesus (see John 3:5-7; 2 Corinthians 5:17).

It's really important to understand that when we're tempted to sin, the temptation can come from Satan or the world—or many times, even from ourselves. Now, this is an idea that you'll rarely hear from people today. In today's culture people say things such as "We're basically good." "We can change ourselves and fix our own problems because we're smart enough." But the Bible tells us in James 1:13-15 that we shouldn't blame God when we're tempted. It's not God who tempts us, but our own evil desires.

The apostle Paul was called Saul before his conversion. He was psycho! His job was attacking the followers of Christ (see Acts 7:57, 58; 8:1, 3; and 9:1, 2)! On Saul's way to Damascus he had a personal encounter with Jesus that led to his conversion (see Acts 9:1-22). Obviously at that point, he put his psycho days behind him, but he still struggled between his natural self (flesh) and God's Holy Spirit.

Paul describes his struggle with sin in Romans 7:14-25, basically saying that he wants to do the right thing, but there is another power working in him that fights against God's Holy Spirit. So the good stuff that he wants to do, he doesn't do, and the bad stuff that he doesn't want to do, he does. We've all felt like Paul, haven't we? Maybe you're feeling this way right now.

But the solution is simple: kill the natural sinful self! Now, don't freak out. This is God's solution to the sin problem, not mine.

The Bible tells us that Jesus Christ died in our place to take the penalty for our sins. He was perfect and sinless, and He *became sin for us* (see 2 Corinthians 5:21). Yeah, I know; I still can't understand that completely either. Paul explains it like this in Galatians 2:20: "My old self has been crucified with Christ. It is no longer I who live, but Christ lives in me. So I live in this earthly body by trusting in the Son of God, who loved me and gave himself for me" (NLT).

Did you catch that? Paul says that when he accepted Christ's death by faith as a payment for his sin, his natural, sinful old self was crucified (and died) with Christ, and the person who is alive now in Paul's body isn't Paul, but Jesus! I know it's confusing. Read Romans 6:1-14 for further clarification.

So how does this work out in real life? Well, simply put, each day you have to kill your old sinful self . . . again and again and again some days. At the beginning of each new day, remind yourself that the sinful old you is dead. Instead, Jesus is in charge—but only as long as you choose for Him to be. God created us with total freedom. We get to decide whether to love and serve Him or not. But if we do choose Him, then we have to give ourselves to Him *completely*. Surrendering our will to God so that He can call the shots is the easiest—and also the most difficult—thing we'll ever do. Every day we'll have to make the decision all over again to die to self. We'll be "dead men and women walking" for God!

Jesus said: "If any of you wants to be my follower, you must turn from your selfish ways, take up your cross daily, and follow me. If you try to hang on to your life, you will lose it. But if you give up your life for my sake, you will save it" (Luke 9:23, 24, NLT).

So let's go back to the question that began all this: How is it possible for you and me to truly love God and others with all that we've got? The answer is that we can't—but God can.

SIMPLE?

God has given us eternal life, and this life is in his Son. Whoever has the Son has life; whoever does not have the Son of God does not have life" (1 John 5:11, 12, NIV).

I'm constantly amazed that when many people—even Christians—hear this verse, they get bothered, upset, offended, and even angry! When the apostle John wrote this, his goal wasn't to be mean, intolerant, or disrespectful. He was simply stating a reality of life. To make sure you don't miss this profoundly important truth, here it is: If you have accepted Jesus' offer to switch His life for yours, then you've got eternal life. If you haven't done this, then all you have is eternal death.

It would be silly to get upset with somebody and call them an intolerant bigot if all they tried to do is warn you that if you went scuba diving without a tank of air, you would die. If a doctor told you that if you didn't take a specific medicine for your illness, you would die, why would you get angry? The doc is just stating a simple fact! The same is true with our relationship with Jesus. John, who knew Jesus personally, says it like this: "In him was life, and that life was the light of all mankind" (John 1:4, NIV). Here's John's equation: Jesus = life! Simple, right? Wrong!

There are many people today who want to split hairs, make excuses, and ask all kinds of convoluted questions to complicate this issue when it really is quite straightforward and simple. The question we all have to ask ourselves today—and hopefully ask others as well—is this: Do you have Jesus?

How can you actually *have* somebody? OK, I'll admit that it's a difficult concept to explain. Let me ask it another way: Does Jesus *have* you? You know what I mean, don't you? This is the difference between knowing about Jesus and knowing Jesus. This is the difference between asking "Would doing __________ be breaking any commandments or rules?" versus asking "Would doing ___________ take me further from Jesus or draw me closer to Him?" It's the difference between a "How much can I get away with and still slide into heaven by the skin of my teeth?" attitude versus an "I hate things that will hurt my relationship with Jesus, and I want to stay as far away from sin as I possibly can" attitude.

Many people see Jesus simply as a ticket to stay out of hell. Jesus has been jokingly called "the ultimate fire insurance." But Jesus tells us Himself that there will be people who think that they have Jesus, when in fact they don't. Jesus made this very scary statement: "Not everyone who says to me, 'Lord, Lord,' will enter the kingdom of heaven, but only the one who does the will of my Father who is in heaven. Many will say to me on that day, 'Lord, Lord, did we not prophesy in your name and in your name drive out demons and in your name perform many miracles?' Then I will tell them plainly, 'I never knew you. Away from me, you evildoers!' " (Matthew 7:21-23, NIV). Jesus clearly states that not only does He not know all the people who did good things in His name, but He *never knew them.*

So how do we keep ourselves from being members of this shocked group of people who will be headed to an eternity without Jesus? How do we keep from fooling not just others but ourselves? The answer lies in a deeper study of the same passage from which we got Jesus' shocking statement: "Enter through the narrow gate. For wide is the gate and broad is the road that leads to destruction, and many enter through it. But small is the gate and narrow the road that leads to life, and only a few find it. Watch out for false prophets. They come to you in sheep's clothing, but inwardly they are ferocious wolves. By their fruit you will recognize them. Do people pick grapes from thornbushes, or figs from thistles? Likewise, every good tree bears good fruit, but a bad tree bears bad fruit. A good tree cannot bear bad fruit, and a bad tree cannot bear good fruit. Every tree that does not bear good fruit is cut down and thrown into the fire. Thus, by their fruit you will recognize them" (verses 13-20, NIV).

Don't miss it: Jesus is saying that not everybody who goes to church is a true Christian. In fact, there are many so-called Christians who do all kinds of wonderful things in the name of Jesus—and those things in themselves aren't bad, but Jesus isn't talking about doing things as the criteria for admittance into heaven. He's talking about choosing to have a real, vibrant, daily relationship with Him.

Did you notice that He talked about choosing between the narrow and wide roads? He wasn't just talking about non-Christians choosing the wide road. That verse was talking about Christians! He was saying that you can call yourself a Christian all day long, but walking "the straight and narrow"—this is where that term comes from—means that you have to let go of a lot of stuff. Because the road is narrow, there's room for only you and Jesus—nothing or nobody else!

Jesus clearly states that if people call themselves a Christian, a good way for us to know if they really are one is simply to pay attention to their life. Anybody can be good and do good things during church, or do good things in the name of the church or even in the name of Jesus. But a closer examination of their life will reveal what they're made of. What do they listen to and watch? How do they talk? What kinds of jokes do they tell? What do they laugh at? How do they spend their money and time? How do they treat their family and friends? What kind of employee are they?

Jesus used this same word picture of tree and fruit while talking about the spiritual leaders of His day and how they looked holy, but in actuality were hypocrites because the words they spoke revealed what was truly in their hearts. He told them: "Make a tree good and its fruit will be good, or make a tree bad and its fruit will be bad, for a tree is recognized by its fruit" (Matthew 12:33, NIV).

So if you truly care about your relationship with Jesus and don't want to fool yourself into thinking you've got life when in actuality you don't, here are two suggestions:

Ask God to reveal the true intent of your heart. God says that our hearts are deceitful above all else. Ask God to wake you up. Pray the prayer that David prayed in Psalm 139:23, 24, and then hold on. God will answer. When He brings things to your mind, confess, repent, and obey. Obedience to God paves the way for growing intimacy with Him. Then pray what David prayed in Psalm 51:10, and God will do it.

Ask others for their true and honest opinion of you. And when they tell you, listen and change. Don't be stubborn or prideful or make excuses. Change! Where has doing things your own way gotten you? Proverbs 11:14 warns: "For lack of guidance a nation falls, but victory is won through many advisers" (NIV).

Someone a long time ago said the same thing that John said about Jesus. You've likely seen it on billboards, church signs, T-shirts, and bumper stickers. The philosopher stated: "Know Jesus, know peace. No Jesus, no peace!" Here's to a purposeful, powerful, and peaceful life of knowing Jesus. It's really that simple.

IS YOUR JESUS USED UP AND BROKEN DOWN?

When my son was born, he received two very special gifts. One was a small blue blanket with his name embroidered on it, and the other was a very soft teddy bear. He liked the blanket, but it stayed in his crib, and he used it only at night. But his little teddy bear was a whole different story. He loved to sleep with it, eat with it, play with it, go to the bathroom with it, and drag it around the house, outside, in the car, to church . . . He took that bear everywhere with him. We had to draw the line at bathtime—the bear was not going swimming! But rest assured that the bear wasn't very far away as it waited for him, guarding his towel from would-be thieves.

When it was time for sleep, woe be unto you if that teddy bear wasn't in the crib with him as he lay down for a nap or at bedtime! I can still remember peeking in on him and seeing him with that bear in a choke hold. It was either under one of his arms or right next to his face. It had to be touching him, or he had to be touching it! Very quickly it became worn-out and threadbare, but he didn't care. He still loved that thing with every fiber of his being.

Did I mention that it also became very nasty very quickly and had to be washed very often? You would think that an asleep toddler wouldn't notice a missing bear for an hour or two right after a long day of . . . toddling. But if the bear was missing, my boy sounded the alarm. He wasn't having that at all. So my wife and I did what any self-respecting grown person would do: when it went to the washer, we replaced it with a similar toy.

However, my son was not fooled so easily. One time after he went to bed I waited the requisite amount of time until I knew he was good and asleep (thank you, baby monitor). Then I snuck into his room, and—like Indiana Jones, nervous and sweating, standing before the little pudgy golden statue with a bag of sand in one hand—I gingerly and gently slid the bear out from my son's boa-constrictor grip and replaced it with the decoy. So far, so good! As I turned to leave his room, he stirred and sat bolt upright, eyes wide open. I don't have to tell you what came next. His "midnight cry" was so loud that he woke up his big sister and my wife! My son is fine now, but that bear is in his hope chest for him to share with his children and his children's children.

You may think this story is a funny little anecdote about my son's early years, but it raises a larger, more poignant question: "What does your Jesus look like?" Is He barely used and in pristine condition, like my son's blanket? Do you see Him once a day—or once a week at church? Or is your Jesus used up and broken down, like my son's bear? Do you take Him everywhere you go and can't stand to be apart from Him—even for a moment?

In the morning as your eyes open, do you, like King David, proclaim "My soul finds rest in God" (Psalm 62:1, NIV) and "You, God, are my God, earnestly I seek you; I thirst for you, my whole being longs for you, in a dry and parched land where there is no water" (Psalm 63:1, NIV)? As you're preparing for and planning your day, is your prayer "Satisfy us in the morning with your unfailing love, that we may sing for joy and be glad all our days" (Psalm 90:14, NIV)? Throughout the day, is your prayer "Oh, how I love your law! I meditate on it all day long" (Psalm 119:97, NIV)? At night, as you lay down to sleep, is your prayer "Your decrees are the theme of my song wherever I lodge. In the night, Lord, I remember your name, that I may keep your law" (Psalm 119:54, 55, NIV)?

I earnestly hope and pray that today you, like the apostle Paul, will take time to deepen your resolve as you recognize that "Nothing is as wonderful as knowing Christ Jesus my Lord. I have given up everything else and count it all as garbage. All I want is Christ and to know that I belong to him. . . . All I want is to know Christ and the power that raised him to life" (Philippians 3:8-10).

I promise you: a life invested in seeking to know Jesus better and better every day will yield a deeper, richer Christian experience and a peaceful, purposeful, and powerful life. And one day, when you see Jesus face to face, you can thank Him for the gift of His Holy Spirit (John 14:15-26) that assured you that He could be used up and broken down.

MERRY CHRISTMAS . . . I CLEANED UP YOUR MESS!

Aaagggghhhhhh!" We all heard a scream and a crash.

My daughter and I rushed into the dining room to find that my son had dropped oatmeal all over himself and the floor. My son stood there in shock. My daughter, exasperated at her little brother (or her "little bother," as she calls him) shook her finger in his face and said, "Look at the mess you've made!"

I quickly shooed my son to his room to change his clothes. As he and I returned to clean up the mess on the dining room floor, we both heard my daughter sweetly say, "Merry Christmas, Jackson. I cleaned up your mess!"

I laughed out loud, but then I got very quiet and began to cry softly as the weight of those words washed over me like a tidal wave.

You see, on a Christmas night some 2,000 years ago, in a little no-name town, a no-name teenage mother had a baby. He was born in a dark, drafty, filthy, stinky, cold barn. Here's how John explains it: "In the beginning was the one who is called the Word. The Word was with God and was truly God. From the very beginning the Word was with God. And with this Word, God created all things. Nothing was made without the Word. Everything that was created received its life from him, and his life gave light to everyone. . . . The Word became a human being and lived here with us. We saw his true glory, the glory of the only Son of the Father. From him all the kindness and all the truth of God have come down to us" (John 1:1-14).

God came down to be with us. When Jesus was born, it was God's way of saying to the human race, "Look at the mess you've made by sinning and turning your back on God, but merry Christmas—I cleaned up your mess!"

John goes on to tell us: "God loved the people of this world so much that he gave his only Son, so that everyone who has faith in him will have eternal life and never really die. God did not send his Son into the world to condemn its people. He sent him to save them!" (John 3:16, 17).

I'm so glad that God came into this world not just to point out our mess, but to clean it up. He did this by being born as a helpless little baby, living a perfect life, dying a sinner's death (though perfect), and finally being raised to life.

Merry Christmas! Jesus has cleaned up the mess you can't clean up for yourself. So live your life for Him and make sure that when you come across others who've made a mess of their lives, let them know that Jesus died to clean up their mess as well.

"YOU'RE NOT MY DADDY!"

"You're not my daddy! You're not my daddy!" My daughter screamed hysterically and ran out of the room.

I stood there in shock, letting her reaction to my new look sink in. You see, my 11-year-old daughter had never seen me without facial hair. And in the 17 years that my wife and I had known each other, she had seen me in this disgraceful state only once.

It all started a few years ago when I turned 40. In my midlife crisis, I decided to grow a full beard in addition to my goatee—a move that was looked upon with derision by my wife and daughter. My wife decided to speak to me about it, but I put my foot down, dug in my heels, and boldly charged forward.

Fast-forward two months. Now my beard was in the fullness of its glory. Don't ask me why, but that's when I decided to shave my head and beard, but keep my goatee.

Things were going well until I sneezed. Normally that wouldn't be such a big deal, but I happened to have the clippers in my hand while trimming the hair around my beard. In retrospect, I probably should have used my trimmer or my scissors, but I didn't think they were up to the task of the thickness of my facial hair. Imagine trying to chop down a California redwood tree with a butter knife (OK, maybe I'm exaggerating . . . a little).

So there I was, standing in front of my bathroom mirror, now looking as though my elevator didn't go all the way to the top. So I decided to just shave everything off. As I did it, I couldn't have anticipated my family's overwhelming negative responses. Even as I write this, my daughter is staring at me across the kitchen table, like a fish from the pet store would respond to its new owner's home: *It looks like my old tank . . . It's got glass walls, water, rocks, and other fish . . . But something just ain't right!*

Something just ain't right! That's a great way to explain our responses to what we perceive God to be like while we live in this sin-sick world. Try as we may, we'll never be able to experience, understand, and know God clearly, fully, and perfectly—as He sees, understands, and knows us. The apostle Paul said it best when he wrote: "Now all we can see of God is like a cloudy picture in a mirror. Later *we will see him face to face.* We don't know everything, *but then we will*, just as God completely understands us" (1 Corinthians 13:12).

So we strive every day to know Him better, to know Him more. No one put it more clearly than that same apostle when he wrote: "Nothing is as wonderful as knowing Christ Jesus my Lord. I have given up everything else and count it all as garbage. *All I want is Christ* and to know that I belong to him. . . . *All I want is to know Christ* and the power that raised him to life" (Philippians 3:8-10).

As frustrating as this present reality is, we can thank God that this isn't all there is. There is something—no, *Someone*—so much better. A guy named Job, who many years ago got a bum rap, understood this principle about as clearly as anybody. (I find it interesting that many times people who have the most wisdom about life are those who are dying or close to it.) Job, in the midst of devastating illness and personal loss, was able to see so clearly. It blows me away that he had this keen insight. Through his anger, questions, grief, loss, and pain, he verbalized both the utter helplessness of every human and the ultimate hope of every Christian: "I know that my Savior lives, and at the end he will stand on this earth. My flesh may be destroyed, yet from this body *I will see God.* Yes, *I will see him for myself,* and I long for that moment" (Job 19:25-27).

I long for that moment too, don't you? Can you imagine it—finally seeing Jesus face to face? We can try, but Paul tells us that we truly can't or won't be able to fathom what that moment will be like. He tried to wrap his mind around it by describing it to the Christians in Corinth, Greece, when he wrote: "What God has planned for people who love him is more than eyes have seen or ears have heard. It has never even entered our minds!" (1 Corinthians 2:9).

Paul pulls back the curtain of all our feeble earthly reality when he tells us about what he admittedly calls "a mystery": "Not every one of us [Christians] will die, but we will all be changed. It will happen suddenly, quicker than the blink of an eye. At the sound of the last trumpet the [righteous] dead will be raised. We will all be changed, so that we will never die again" (1 Corinthians 15:51, 52).

Some Christians are bothered or scared by things they can't understand, but I can't wait. The Bible gives us information about what heaven will be like, but the part that interests me the most is not what it will look like or even where it is, but who will be there. Jesus, as He was preparing His disciples for the difficulties that lay ahead of them, reassured them with these words: "Don't be worried! *Have faith in God and have faith in me.* There are many rooms in my Father's house. I wouldn't tell you this, unless it was true. I am going there to prepare a place for each of you. After I have done this, *I will come back and take you with me. Then we will be together*" (John 14:1-3). The promise He made to His disciples more than 2,000 years ago still rings true today.

John, that same disciple who was present when Jesus made that promise and wrote down Jesus' words, was also the same one who—much older—saw in vision the fulfillment of that promise. Thank God that he wrote it down for us in order to bring us encouragement and strength in this time in earth's history: "The angel showed me a river that was crystal clear, and its waters gave life. The river came from the throne where God and the Lamb were seated. . . . God's curse will no longer be on the people of that city. *He and the Lamb will be seated there on their thrones, and its people will worship God and will see him face to face.* God's name will be written on the foreheads of the people. . . . Then I was told: *These words are true and can be trusted*" (Revelation 22:1-6).

Imagine how he must have felt immediately after receiving this vision and having the words the angel had just told him—"These words are true and can be trusted"—echoing in his head. Then suddenly and powerfully these words connected in his memory to those beautiful, reassuring words that Jesus had told him so many years before: "Have faith in me. . . . I wouldn't tell you this, unless it was true. . . . I will come back and take you with me. Then we will be together" (John 14:1-3). Wow!

God says these same words to you and me today. He tells us that no matter who we are, where we are, what we've done, what we're doing, what's happening, or what's happened, we can know—we can be reassured—that even though today we may feel far away from God, there will come a time when you and I, and the world, will see, experience, and know Him for who He truly is.

It is my prayer that all of us will be ready and excited to see Him face to face and will respond with joy and expectation. What a day that will be when we can all say the words written by the prophet Isaiah: "The Lord All-Powerful will destroy the power of death and wipe away all tears. No longer will his people be insulted everywhere. The Lord has spoken! At that time, people will say, 'The Lord has saved us! Let's celebrate. We waited and hoped—now our God is here' " (Isaiah 25:8, 9). We will, in effect, call God our heavenly Father.

The only other response to the most wonderful and blessed event of Jesus' return will sadly be like my daughter's anguished cries of "You're not my daddy! You're not my daddy!" John the revelator had a vision of what this would be like as well. He tells us that many people will respond to this event with utter dread, shock, terror, and horror: "Then the sky was rolled up like a scroll, and all mountains and islands were moved from their places. The kings of the earth, its famous people, and its military leaders hid in caves or behind rocks on the mountains. They hid there together with the rich and the powerful and with all the slaves and free people. Then they shouted to the mountains and the rocks, 'Fall on us! *Hide us* from the one who sits on the throne and from the anger of the Lamb. That terrible day has come! God and the Lamb will show their anger, and *who can face it*?' " (Revelation 6:14-17).

When my daughter ran out of the room screaming, I didn't find it funny or entertaining at all. I was worried about her. If that was my response to my daughter, what do you think God feels when you and I consistently respond negatively to His offers of peace, life, love, and a forever relationship with Him? The Old Testament prophet Ezekiel gives us a hint of the heart of God when he writes that God says, "I don't like to see wicked people die. I enjoy seeing them turn from their sins and live" (Ezekiel 33:11).

So I ask each one of you: What will your response be to God's forever offer? Will you gladly and confidently respond, "You're my Daddy," or will your response be the cry of shock, terror, and awe: "You're not my Daddy"?

THERE'S NOTHING YOU CAN DO TO MAKE ME STOP LOVING YOU

As the father of two very different children—one of them really strong-willed—I definitely understand the frustration that God feels with me when I continue to sin and take His love and protection for granted. But God has never given up on me, and I know that He loves me no matter what I do.

My love for my children is the same. It isn't based on anything they do but on the fact that they're my children. You see, there's nothing they can do to make me stop loving them. Every night after I pray with them and tuck them in, I say to them the simple yet powerful words that all of us long to hear: "There's nothing you can do . . ." And they finish the familiar statement: ". . . to make me stop loving you!"

This is especially important for them to know when I'm disciplining them. There's no more powerful time for me to remind them that my love for them isn't dependent on them.

In the Bible God did the same thing by reminding His children, the Israelites, that He loved them supremely—even in the midst of having to discipline them in the form of being attacked and enslaved by many different nations. God never stopped loving them or reminding them of this fact. In Jeremiah 31:3 God said: "I have loved you with an everlasting love; I have drawn you with unfailing kindness" (NIV). And in Deuteronomy 7:9 God says: "Know therefore that the Lord your God is God; he is the faithful God, keeping his covenant of love to a thousand generations of those who love him and keep his commandments" (NIV).

So when you mess up big-time and you think you've blown it so badly that nothing can be repaired, remember that God loves you and that He'll never stop. And if He loves you and me enough to send His Son, Jesus, to die for us, how could we ever choose not to love Him back? How could we ever choose to turn away from so great a love? If you haven't chosen to accept God's love today, don't wait another minute. It'll be the best decision of your life.

THE COSMIC CONFLICT

The Super Bowl is about the two best teams in pro football going at it head to head. You expect there to be a showdown of epic proportions! Each team gives its all to win.

This brings to mind the fact that there are two cosmic "teams" currently battling to the death. What they're fighting for is far more monumental than the Super Bowl trophy; it's nothing less than the hearts and minds of every human being on Planet Earth. God and His followers are locked in mortal combat with Satan and his followers—good versus evil.

How did this all start? Basically, God made Satan, but when he was in heaven his name was Lucifer and he was second in charge (see Ezekiel 28:12-17). The Old Testament prophet Isaiah gives more details about the pride and jealousy that Satan initiated and nurtured in himself, changing him from the sinless being that God had created into the first sinful being in the universe (see Isaiah 14:12-15).

So Satan, in his desire to be equal with God, began to undermine God by spreading among the other angels the first rumors and lies ever told in the universe—lies about God's character. Satan began cunningly hinting to the other angels that God was unfair, selfish, unjust, and holding them back from complete freedom to do as they wished.

God was patient with Satan and gave him chance after chance to repent and return to his exalted position in the heavenly family. But Satan stubbornly persisted in his rebellion and was so successful with his lying accusations against the character of God that he convinced large numbers of the angels in heaven to rebel with him. The Bible tells us what happened next: "And war broke out in heaven: Michael [another name for Christ] and his angels fought with the dragon; and the dragon and his angels fought, but they did not prevail, nor was a place found for them in heaven any longer. So the great dragon was cast out, that serpent of old, called the Devil and Satan, who deceives the whole world; he was cast to the earth, and his angels were cast out with him" (Revelation 12:7-9, NKJV).

The great controversy between good and evil began then and continues to this day. What are God and Satan fighting over? The allegiance of every human being! God desires our love and loyalty. He wants us to choose the free gifts of salvation and eternal life. He longs to be our heavenly Father: "But as many as received Him [Christ], to them He gave the right to become children of God" (John 1:12, NKJV).

Satan, on the other hand, will do whatever it takes to keep us sinning so that we'll be eternally lost. Misery loves company, and after Satan was thrown out of heaven, his main goal was to drag as many of us down with him as he could! It hurts God to lose even one of us, so Satan wants to torture Him to the max by claiming as many of us as he can. The apostle Peter warns: "Your adversary the devil walks about like a roaring lion, seeking whom he may devour" (1 Peter 5:8, NKJV). The apostle John records: "Woe to the inhabitants of the earth and the sea! For the devil has come down to you, having great wrath, because he knows that he has a short time [before Christ's second coming]" (Revelation 12:12, NKJV).

The apostle Paul describes this cosmic battle that we're caught up in: "We are not fighting against humans. We are fighting against forces and authorities and against rulers of darkness and powers in the spiritual world" (Ephesians 6:12). How can we overcome such foes?

Paul has the awesome answer: that we are to put on the mighty armor of God. He then describes every piece of armor in detail (we'll talk about this in more detail in another chapter). With God's armor we can successfully stop Satan's attack (see Ephesians 6:10-18).

Whenever you're tempted to feel overwhelmed or to wonder whether Satan may win after all, just remember to read the end of the book. Pick up your Bible and turn to Revelation 20:9, 10. It announces that the ultimate victory will belong to God and those who love Him.

For the Super Bowl, everybody likes to pick the winning team, but who can know for sure who will win? Well, in the great battle between good and evil, we can be sure that God will win. The only question is: Will you and I be on the right team?

LIFE'S CURVEBALLS

I don't know what to do, Mr. M! I just don't know what to do." Sheri (not her real name) sat in my office crying and screaming out of control. I jumped up to close the door as the other counselor down the hall popped her head into my office. There she saw a crumpled mass of middle-school girl balled up on my couch surrounded by pillows and stuffed animals. I quickly responded, "We're good," and the other counselor closed my door to give us some privacy.

Sheri had just found out earlier that morning . . . on the way to school . . . via text message . . . from her older sister . . . that her parents were divorcing! So there Sheri sat, sullen, sad, shocked. "Everything in my life is falling apart, Mr. M. I can't believe this is happening. I mean, it's like I'm living in a dream and I'm gonna wake up and it's all gonna be OK . . . I just don't know what to do."

Do you know what great words of wisdom I had for her? None! I said absolutely nothing. What could I possibly say to her at that moment that could make her feel better?

Have you ever been there? Have you ever been the supportive friend or family member who's had to try to put all the pieces back together after a huge life letdown? Has life ever thrown you a curveball? I mean, something that just comes totally out of the blue.

Hey, maybe right now you're not the person who's trying to support the Sheri in your life—maybe you're the Sheri who's just had the wind knocked out of you! Maybe you've gone through a breakup, or your family is falling apart, or you've had a bad doctor's report, or someone you love is in the hospital about to die (or just died), or you're failing a class (or a whole semester). The list could go on and on. How do you deal with it? What are you supposed to do? Is God there? And if He is, does He care? Does the Bible have any answers for you, your family, and your friends that could help you know what to do . . . when you don't know what to do?

God is there. God cares. He tells us that He will never leave us alone—*ever.* And He'll be with us until the world ends (see Matthew 28:20). And the Bible, His love letter to us, shares lots of wonderful stories about love, life, hope, salvation, mercy, and grace. But it also shares lots of not-so-wonderful stories about loss, depression, death, deception . . . well, you get the not-so-pretty picture. The question is: Why? Why doesn't the Bible have just positive, uplifting stories?

The Bible doesn't have stories about just perfect things that happen because life isn't always perfect with rainbows and ponies. Many times life is hard, sad, messy stuff.

I mean, the moment Adam and Eve took a bite of the "forbidden fruit" and sinned, bad things started happening. We were immediately separated from a relationship with God by sin, and things have never been the same since. There were a lot of firsts in the Garden of Eden: the first surgery, first marriage, first lie, first excuse, and first death. It all went downhill pretty fast.

Jesus Himself said this about our experiences on earth: "Here on earth you will have many trials and sorrows. But take heart, because I have overcome the world" (John 16:33, NLT). Translation: If you're a Christian and on the planet called earth, you're going to go through some really tough times. Peter says it like this in 1 Peter 4:12: "Dear friends, don't be surprised or shocked that you are going through testing that is like walking through fire."

With that said, there are four really important things that I want you to understand:

1. God is for you, not against you. He's your biggest fan! He loves you and wants to spend eternity with you, and He wants to start having a relationship with you right now! God wants you to have a life filled with joy, peace, power, and purpose. He's got awesome things in store for you (see John 10:10 and Jeremiah 29:11).
2. There's nothing that happens to you that God hasn't already known about, purposely planned, or actively allowed. God knows what's up. He's all-powerful, all-knowing, and all-present—I'm glad He's on my side (see Psalm 139:16).
3. The devil hates you and is out to get you. The devil would kill you if he had the opportunity (see 1 Peter 5:8 and John 8:44).
4. Not every bad thing that happens to you is because of God or the devil. Sometimes bad stuff happens as a consequence of a stupid choice that you make (or someone else makes). Choices have consequences. For those of you who love math, here's the equation: Good choices = good consequences, and bad choices = bad consequences (see Galatians 6:7, 8).

The world can be a hard, lonely place. So if I were you, I wouldn't travel alone. Ask God today to walk with you—it'll be the smartest thing you've ever done.

WHO YOU ARE AND WHOSE YOU ARE

Here's a question we received at *Insight* magazine and my response: *I just went through my freshman year in high school. I spent most of the year alone, while everyone else had friends. Of course, everyone knew me because it was a small school. People would tell me just to be myself, but they would try to be like everyone else. Some even said that I was sheltered or brainwashed by my parents and just needed some freedom. This caused me to question my identity as a Christian and also my relationship with my parents. How do I cope with this?—In the Middle, 14, Alabama.*

Dear "In the Middle,"

I'm glad you wrote. It's important to let other people know what's going on with you. Before I address your concerns, I want to be sure that I fully understand what they are:

You're concerned because people are acting like hypocrites—telling you to be individualistic but then trying to be like everybody else.

Your friends are telling you that you're sheltered and/or brainwashed by your parents.

You're questioning your identity as a Christian.

You're questioning your relationship with your parents.

In a nutshell: There's nothing wrong with you! I absolutely agree with what you've said—it seems that the people who are telling you just to be yourself but then are acting like everybody else are wrong! You haven't been sheltered or brainwashed by your parents. It sounds as though your parents have been trying to protect you from the harsh realities of life and the ugliness and dangers of this world—and that's a parent's job!

You've got to remember that when you choose God over sin and the world, many people, even your so-called friends, will get upset with you, pressure you to sin, and make fun of you—sometimes even bully you—for making this choice. In the New Testament book of Romans the apostle Paul spoke about evil people who denied the power and position of God and "gave up the truth about God for a lie" (1:25). Later in that chapter (verses 28-32) Paul writes that these types of people aren't kind or caring or respectful of their parents. They're selfish and mean, and all they want to do is evil—and they encourage others to do the same evil and godless things! And when you choose not to join in, they bully and make fun of you. That sounds a lot like the stuff you've been going through.

Take heart. Following God's will and ways will always result in a better, longer, happier life. I'm proud of you for taking a stand for God.

The question still remains: How do you deal with so-called "friends" who try to make you feel like garbage when you don't brainlessly follow along with what they're doing? Well, you first need to understand who you are. But you can't do that until you answer the question of *whose* you are. That's one of those really important kind-of-have-to-know-the answer-before-I-die questions.

Well, whose are you? You're God's child! Check out what Paul wrote in Ephesians 1. Did you notice that Paul says about seven times something like: "You've been chosen by God in Christ Jesus"? We are God's adopted children through Jesus' shed blood on the cross! You and I and all Christians are Christ's body, and we are filled with Him!

Just because you're a Christian doesn't mean that things will be easy for you. In fact, teens fall in love with Jesus, commit their lives to Him, get baptized . . . and then it seems that everything goes haywire. And they can't figure out what's gone wrong. When this happens, sometimes they just stop being Christians. They figure, "This isn't worth the struggle and the pain." But as the Bible says—or maybe it's Chuck Norris—"No pain, no gain!"

In my short but interesting life I've found this to be true: the closer you are to Christ, generally the more difficult your life will be! Not all Christians will have physical persecution—but they will have some sort of persecution. The bottom line is this: If you choose Christ, you'll catch flak. But you'll also have peace.

So that's it? If you're a Christian, you're going to have problems? Well, yes! Don't get upset with me; I didn't say it. Jesus did. Look at John 15:18-21. Before you were a Christian, you were going with the flow. You were doing what the world was doing, talking like the world, dressing like the world, acting like the world. But now as a Christian, what God expects of you and me is totally against the world. We, as Christians, are swimming against the current. Have you ever seen salmon swimming upstream? Is it easy? Of course not!

I know that this is a difficult time for you, but you can get it done by tapping into the power of the Holy Spirit, staying close to Jesus, praying and reading/studying your Bible every day, and hanging out with the right types of friends—even if it means that you have to be a loner.

When it comes to your relationship with your parents, the bottom line is this: When you honor and obey your parents, you're honoring and obeying God as well. What do I mean by honoring? Well, it's not enough to do what your parents tell you to do (obedience); you've got to do it with a right heart attitude. I'm not saying that you've got to want to be 100 percent on board, but you shouldn't be disrespectful and rude to them—and you certainly shouldn't be cursing them or wishing them harm or actually physically or emotionally abusing them. Paul also wrote this to the Ephesians: "Children, you belong to the Lord, and you do the right thing when you obey your parents. The first commandment with a promise says, 'Obey your father and your mother, and you will have a long and happy life' " (Ephesians 6:1, 2).

Isn't that interesting that God says that the result of honoring and obeying your parents is both a long and a happy life? God gave you parents to lead and guide and direct you and help you grow up to be a happy and successful adult. Of course, that doesn't mean that just because your parents are grown they're off the hook any more than you are. Ephesians 6:4 says: "Parents, don't be hard on your children. Raise them properly. Teach them and instruct them about the Lord."

As Christians, we've all got specific jobs to do to help us all get through this life with a minimum of bumps along the way, and when we honor and obey one another—brothers and sisters included—we go a long way to living a happier, healthier, and longer life and showing the world that life as a Christian really works. And in the end, the world will notice something different, so go ahead and be different!

As the old hymn says, "Stand up, stand up for Jesus!" I promise you, Jesus will be right there standing beside you all the way to heaven. He's faithful, and He won't ever let you down.

DIRTY DIAPERS AND DIFFICULT DAILY DECISIONS

Boo-boo!" my 2½-year-old son ran up to me screaming. He was frantically clawing at his diaper, squirming, and jumping up and down. We were in the throes of potty training, and "boo-boo" from Jackson meant "poo-poo."

I picked him up as carefully as I could, already thinking about how I would deal with the disastrous results of his efficient and apparently powerful little digestive system. I ran to the bathtub and placed him in it. I peeled his shirt and pants off him. Then I took a towel and wiped him off as much as I could. I then proceeded to take Jackson to his changing table, aka decontamination area, and win my Daddy points for the day.

I prepared myself for the worst. I quickly tried to take off my son's diaper. He allowed me to undo one side of the diaper but began to cry and scream hysterically when I tried to get the other off. I was confused. I tried forcing it off, but my son just grabbed my fingers with his hands and twisted them backward . . . ow!

So I in all my wisdom began to explain to my son why he should let Daddy take off his diaper. I picked up a clean diaper and some baby powder and began: "Jackson, look what Daddy has! That's right, it's a clean diaper and some baby powder. You have a nasty, stinky booty, and Daddy wants to clean you up. I know that you don't want to be yucky. Just let Daddy clean you up, and then you'll be sweet and clean, and we can go play."

My son wasn't buying it. In fact, he stopped crying, looked me dead in the eyes, locked his knees in the fetal position, and screamed, "No! Mine!"

I was beside myself. I didn't know what to do. I thought to myself, *Why isn't my son letting me near him? He's the one who initially came to me and told me that he was dirty. Why is he being so stubborn? He's acting like he can do this all by himself, but he can't. He's too young. All I want to do is to make him clean, but he won't let me!*

At that moment a little voice in my head said, "Now you understand!" God had spiritually knocked me down—yet again! I finally got it. It took another minute, but my son *finally* allowed me to change his diaper, and we went on with our day. But what God taught me still resounds with me. You see, I am learning a lot about my own sinful, stubborn, stained character as the father of a child who's just like me.

Forget the romantic notion of God speaking to Moses from the burning bush or speaking to the Israelites from Mount Sinai; no, God got hold of my heart right there in front of my son's changing table! It took my son and me battling over who would have control of making him clean. I'm a recovering sinner, and like all sinners, I have a hard time letting go and letting God. I constantly struggle with my will. I learned three valuable lessons that day:

1. Knowing that I have sin in my life doesn't make it go away. My son

informed me that he had a dirty diaper, but that didn't help the filth to be cleaned, did it?

2. I can't clean myself up, no matter how much I try or how much I want to.
3. God can want me to get clean all day long, but until I decide to stop fighting and let Him clean me, it won't happen.

I hope you've learned some powerful and important lessons about giving God your heart and will. The apostle Paul said it best when he said: "I die daily" (1 Corinthians 15:31, NKJV). Even when we don't know what to say or how to say it, we can still ask God to help us to give Him our heart and mind every day. Never forget: God is in the business of changing hearts and minds for the better.

SAY "UNCLE!"

When I was a kid, I used to get into all kinds of fights with my two brothers—over all kinds of silly stuff. The fights didn't last long, and the bigger sibling usually won (not me). Traditionally the loser wouldn't be released until he admitted defeat. More times than not, I was told by a brother who was on top of me, holding me down, "Say 'uncle!' " So I did, because if I didn't, I'd probably still be there to this day!

God wants us to say the same thing to Him. Not that He's beating us down and yelling at us to submit. Rather, He's asking us to give up trying to do things on our own. He wants to help us. He wants us to realize that we can't save ourselves, and when we realize this and let Him take control, awesome things happen!

In previous chapters we've talked about accepting a relationship with Jesus Christ in order to receive the peace, love, and acceptance that we were made for. There's a definite connection between obedience and submission, but submission is different from obedience. Obedience is the *act* of obeying, and submission is the *attitude* of obedience.

If someone threatened me with death if I didn't obey them, I would obey. This is not so with submission. Someone who has submitted wants to obey; they don't have to be forced or threatened. When we talk about submitting to God, we're talking about willing obedience that springs out of our love and thankfulness to Him.

Obedience is difficult for a sinner born into sin. Everything starts with our attitude. But we as sinful humans need an attitude adjustment. We need to exchange our attitude for the attitude of Christ. The apostle Paul in his letter to the Christians in Philippi writes about this (see Philippians 2:1-13). This passage speaks about having a super-close relationship with God. Again we see the distinct connection between loving God and loving others as a response to God. Paul also discusses the importance of humility, with Jesus as our example. Jesus didn't put His needs above our own, but became humble to God, obeying Him and even dying as a criminal on a cross!

Humility will allow us to draw closer to God because we get ourselves out of the way, and then God is able to use us in any way He wants to. At the end of this passage we see an important principle: God's power makes it possible for us to want to make positive changes in our lives, and it is that same power that makes it possible for us to change. This is the importance of submitting our will to God. He, working in us, begins and completes the process of making us perfect (sanctification).

James, the writer of the biblical book by the same name, stresses that we must submit to God in order to resist the devil (see James 4:6-10). There is power in humility and submission. Humility is the internal attitude that allows an individual to be externally submitted. Don't you find it interesting that a Christian can receive power from giving it up? How is that possible? The key to the whole shebang is finding the right person to submit to. God is the right person, and when you submit to Him, all kinds of wonderful things can and will happen. The first is that you will begin to see that you can get free from habits, addictions, and sins that you could never stop by yourself.

Let's take a closer look at the passage in James. There's an important progression that you need to be aware of:

1. God can and will give you the power of the Holy Spirit to overcome all evil—whether the evil comes from you, the devil, or the world—but you've first got to . . .
2. Submit to God. You can say "No" or "Stop" to the devil all you want to, but the reality is that you're about as significant to him as a fly. The devil wants to steal, kill, and destroy (John 10:10), so he's not your friend. You can't resist him by yourself. But once you submit to God and He moves you under His protection and authority, you will be able to say no to the devil. When this happens . . .

3. The devil will flee from you. Without God you were as powerful as a fly, but when God has your back, Satan runs away! But he'll be back—and soon—with a slicker, sneakier temptation. So what do you do?
4. Come close to God, every moment of every day, and God will come close to you. Have you ever been scared of something and then had your parent, sibling, or friend "back you up"? How did you feel? Invincible and untouchable, right? That's exactly what drawing close to God can and will do for you, but you've got to start that process. So how do you remain in that attitude of coming close to God? Well, you . . .
5. Recognize that you're a sinner in need of a Savior. Also, have a serious and realistic recognition of how your attitude, behaviors, and sin affect God deeply and break your relationship with Him. Admit to what you've done wrong with no excuses and say you're sorry (confession) and stop doing it (repentance). When you do that . . .
6. You will have a humble attitude that will put you in a position of submission, which allows God to lift you up to a closer and closer relationship with Him. The process continues every moment of every day, and you will continually draw closer and closer to Him so He can continue making you more and more perfect and sinless (sanctification).

I want to tell you a sad but important story from the Bible that has to do with one knucklehead who decided to learn about submission to God the hard way. We'll also talk about what we can learn from it.

This story illustrates what happens when somebody consistently doesn't submit to God. It's found in Daniel 4, and it's an amazing story of King Nebuchadnezzar—King Nebbi, for short.

Before you read this story, there's something you have to understand about King Nebbi and his culture: they ascribed the status of a god to their king. And as with anything, if you hear something enough times, you begin to believe it (that's why you've got to be careful about your media choices and whom you choose to hang with). So it wasn't a surprise that Nebbi began to believe that he was a god.

God said in the first commandment: "You shall have no other gods before Me" (Exodus 20:3, NKJV). And we read in Scripture that God isn't in the business of sharing His glory with other gods. These are important facts to remember as we consider the lessons and principles of the story in Daniel 4. Read it for yourself, and then we'll discuss what we can learn from Nebbi's mistakes.

So what's the point of this story? That we are to give honor and glory to no one other than God. We are to recognize that by His hand He created all things, controls all things, and gives us our very breath and heartbeat! God doesn't mind if we admire beauty and power, but He wants us to give Him all the credit. After all, He rightfully deserves it. By doing this, we are submitting to His authority and not our own.

I believe that Nebbi learned his lesson and learned true humility. Just the fact that he was able to write this information down gives evidence of this. Yet I find it interesting that even after having been clearly warned by God through the prophet Daniel of what would happen if he didn't change his ways, Nebbi still went down the path of pride. About 12 months later he got an even more serious wake-up call, which shows us our first principle: You and I must choose every day to submit to God, and we must remain vigilant that we don't stray off of the path into taking credit for the good things in our lives. It all comes from God and belongs to God, and He can choose to give it and take it away at any time.

It took seven years for Nebbi to finally humble himself and submit to God! The Bible says that Nebbi prayed, and when he did, his "mind was healed" (Daniel 4:34). In other words, he had lost his mind before he finally humbled himself! Now, what happens when your mind is sick? All kinds of stuff: anxiety, depression, hallucinations, delusions, and other mental health problems.

You might be thinking, "Seven years? Come on, that seems a little extreme for someone to keep living like a wild animal and not to recognize that God's in charge." Oh, really? I wish I would have gotten it after only seven years—it took me longer than that. And I'm sure some of you know people who've been living crazy, out-of-control lives longer than that. Maybe that person is you!

Let me tell you something—when a person continues to live apart from God, their own sin nature, the world, and the devil begin to take over their mind. When that happens, people lose their sense and their conscience (which is from God), and they begin to do more and more strange, evil, and twisted things. They're living only for themselves; they've placed their own needs, wants, and desires above everybody else. The Bible says a lot about this in Romans 1:21-32.

This passage of Scripture describes people who refuse to recognize that God is in charge even in the midst of overwhelming proof, and so God steps back and allows their evil, selfish, violent, sadistic, deranged, sick, and twisted minds and lives to follow the only natural direction they can go without God: straight down.

Does this sound like anybody you know? Maybe you see some of these character traits in yourself. This is the kind of culture that we're living in today. How sad it must be for people who don't acknowledge that God is in control of it all. They will never find true love, joy, or peace. That's why they continue to spin out of control—because they're searching (remember Saul?)

Psalm 36:1-4 says: "Sinners don't respect God; sin is all they think about. They like themselves too much to hate their own sins or even to see them. They tell deceitful lies, and they don't have the sense to live right. Those people stay awake, thinking up mischief, and they follow the wrong road, refusing to turn from sin." Take a cue from King Nebbi and don't go there.

So what's it going to be? Will you choose to honor yourself above God and live a miserable, out-of-control life full of selfishness, pain, and passing pleasure—and then die? Or will you choose to humble yourself before God and recognize that He's in charge, order your life accordingly, then live a life of joy, peace, and contentment both here and in the world to come—and never die? The choice is yours.

GOD WANTS US TO EAT MEAT

When did you become a Christian? When you were a kid? A couple of years ago? This year? This month? Maybe today? Whenever you made the decision, I hope that you're growing spiritually in your relationship with Jesus and in your knowledge about Him, about living a Christian life, and about sharing Jesus with others. If you're not doing any of these things, then you're a *baby!* Hold up! Don't get upset with me; that's what the Bible calls you.

If you're growing spiritually every day, great! But don't stop; there's always room for improvement. Let's look at a couple of scriptures that speak to this issue and see what they have to say about being a baby versus being mature, what that means, what lessons we can learn, and how we can apply them to our lives.

First Corinthians 3:1-3 says: "My friends, you are acting like the people of this world. That's why I could not speak to you as spiritual people. You are like babies as far as your faith in Christ is concerned. So I had to treat you like babies and feed you milk. You could not take solid food, and you still cannot, because you are not yet spiritual. You are jealous and argue with each other. This proves that you are not spiritual and that you are acting like the people of this world."

Wow! Paul really let the Corinthian Christians have it—with both barrels! What could have been happening with them that he had to be so bold? Well, the bottom line was that everybody in the church in Corinth was arguing because some members liked Pastor Paul and others liked Pastor Apollos, and the church was becoming divided because of it. Isn't it interesting that nothing changes in history? I'm sure that there are some Bible teachers that you like better than others, but Paul's response was twofold:

1. It's not about the teacher; it's about Jesus. Jesus is what's important.
2. The Corinthians were acting like non-Christians and spiritual babies.

Instead of being able to talk to these Christians in a mature way, Paul had to remind them that they were "not yet spiritual." How about you? Are there attitudes and actions that you're choosing that are making Jesus say to you, "You're still a spiritual baby"? Is God trying to fatten you up by giving you spiritual solid food or—as other Bible versions call it—"meat"? Are you resisting being fed solid food?

Guess what happens to babies who don't progress from milk to solid food? They don't grow like they should—or worse still, they die! Are you growing in Christ and becoming a mature Christian? Or are you stagnating, doing nothing, and going nowhere spiritually? Or worse still, are you dead?

Let's look at Hebrews 5:12-14: "By now you should have been teachers, but once again you need to be taught the simplest things about what God has said. You need milk instead of solid food. People who live on milk are like babies who don't really know what is right. Solid food is for mature people who have been trained to know right from wrong."

Did you catch Paul inferring that people who are spiritual babies don't know what is right? In fact, he says that the only way for a spiritual baby to know right from wrong is to receive training. I have two young children. My daughter is 11, and my son is almost 7. There are things I allow my daughter to do that I won't allow my son to do. Why? Am I being unfair and mean? Not at all. I don't allow my son to do those things because he is not physically able or doesn't have the brains to do them. He gets really upset and jealous of my daughter's increased freedoms. But he hasn't yet matured the way my daughter has. In fact, if I allowed my son to do them, one of three things would happen:

1. He would get physically injured and/or killed.
2. He would get frustrated because he would consistently fail.
3. He would lose interest quickly because he's not ready for the task.

The best way that I can strengthen and prepare my son to do those things that my daughter can do is to continue feeding him greater and greater amounts of food and to expose him to things that stretch and strengthen his skills. It is only then that he will begin to mature in all his areas enough to do the things that my daughter can do.

You might ask yourself, "What does this have to do with me?" Well, I believe that Paul's metaphor of babies, milk, maturity, and meat applies directly to our spiritual lives. Let me ask you a couple of important questions:

- Are you the kind of person who gets upset that other Christians are doing things that you can't do, or that they appear to have more biblical knowledge than you?
- Do your Christian brothers and sisters seem to be passing you by in their relationship with Jesus? Do they seem to be getting closer and closer to Jesus every day?
- Do your Christian brothers and sisters seem to be gaining victory after victory over difficult areas of their lives, such as certain bad habits, sins, and addictions, and you're not?
- Do you recognize that God is trying to help you mature, but you'd rather stay a baby?
- Is there anything that you are keeping from God that He's asking you to change?

Hebrews 6:1 says: "We must try to become mature and start thinking about more than just the basic things we were taught about Christ. We shouldn't need to keep talking about why we ought to turn from deeds that bring death and why we ought to have faith in God."

God will bless your efforts at maturity if you just try! Just make sure that your motives are right, because if they're not, the changes will not be consistent and long-lasting. If you or someone you know continues to live in the same bad habits, sins, and addictions they had prior to becoming a Christian, this should be a huge red flag that spiritual growth isn't happening.

Remember what Jesus said: "You will know them by their fruits" (Matthew 7:16, NKJV). In other words, people can say a lot of things, but the way that you'll know if they really made a change and are growing as Christians is by their behavior. The Christian life is about peace, power, and overcoming. It's not about stagnation, failure, whining, and complaining. Even if all you're doing is moving forward by baby steps, at least you're moving forward! Before someone can run, they must first learn to crawl.

I've met many people who became Christians decades ago and yet continue to be spiritual babies. They don't tell others about Christ, and they're not active and working in their church; they're just taking up space—like a bump on a log. They're angry, mean, critical, spiteful, unloving, unforgiving, selfish individuals who are stuck in their ways and absolutely refuse to grow!

Now that we've begun to discuss the importance of spiritual maturity, it's time to take your spiritual pulse. What you learn will hopefully reinforce teaching that you've already received and knowledge that you already have. But if not, it may surprise and shock you! If your heart is cold, hard, and dead, it needs a good shock to start beating for Jesus again. Turn up the juice and get the paddles. *Clear!*

SPIRITUAL PHYSICAL

When I was a kid, I hated to have alcohol put on my cuts. It stung! But I knew that in the end, it was for my own good. I endured it because I knew that if I didn't, I might get a serious infection, and the intervention would have to be more severe (also, my father had me in a hammerlock!). Now, get ready for this chapter to sting some. Read, reflect, pray, and change if you need to! Hopefully God won't have to intervene in a more serious way to get your attention (remember King Nebbi?).

Second Corinthians 13:5 says: "Test yourselves and find out if you really are true to your faith. If you pass the test, you will discover that Christ is living in you. But if Christ isn't living in you, you have failed."

Straightforward, isn't it? So have you failed? Do you pass the test?

Here's the bottom line: If Christ is in you, then you're a Christian, and if Christ is not in you, then you're not a Christian.

So how do you know that Christ is in you and you're in Christ? In my own life and in the lives of many other Christians, I have noticed a tendency to relax our collective love and devotion to God. When we first come to Jesus, we are fervent, fiery, and focused. But as life, sin, the devil, and the world take their toll on us, it can be easy to get loose and lazy. So just as it's important to get a physical examination on a consistent basis, it's even more important that we get a spiritual checkup.

Are you ready? Get ready for Jesus to cut deep . . . and when you're in the middle of it all and you're wondering when the pain will end, remember that God is doing it for your own good to give you an authentic, lasting, and eternal relationship with Him.

There are four key questions that you need to keep in mind as you take your spiritual physical:

1. Are you really saved?
2. Have you truly been converted?
3. Can you lose your salvation?
4. Are you daily remaining converted and saved?

I have observed that a true conversion is marked by four distinct attitudes:

1. Obedience to the precepts and principles of right living that God has clearly laid out in the Bible and to what God's Holy Spirit impresses upon your mind;
2. A changed life as observed by confession and repentance of old sinful patterns of living and a replacement of them with right thoughts, motivations, speech, interests, and behaviors;
3. A genuine and sincere motivation and struggle to turn away from those things that would make God sad and to live a life that is marked by obedience to God and a genuine and sincere hatred of the things that God hates;
4. A sober, sorrowful, and broken attitude toward your sin and an immediate confession and repentance in order to minimize hurt and pain toward Jesus and that intimate relationship you share.

In Psalm 119:9-11 the psalmist says: "Young people can live a clean life by obeying your word. I worship you with all my heart. Don't let me walk away from your commands. I treasure your word above all else; it keeps me from sinning against you." The only way we can stay on the "straight and narrow" is to be obedient to the precepts and principles found in God's Word, the Bible. How do we do that? Through serious Bible study and Bible memorization.

Are you studying and memorizing the Bible every day? A little every day goes a long way. You don't need any weird or expensive plans, just a 3″ x 5″ card or a sticky note with a verse or a passage of Scripture on it that you can look at when you have down time, such as when you're standing in line at the grocery store, waiting to see the doc, or just brushing your teeth. (I hope you're brushing your teeth every day . . . eewwwww.)

The psalmist continues by saying: "When I took a long, careful look at your ways, I got my feet back on the trail you blazed. I was up at once, didn't drag my feet, was quick to follow your orders" (Psalm 119:59, 60, Message). Someone who is truly wanting to have a deeper relationship with Jesus will do two things:

1. They will think deeply about what God is saying and examine their thoughts, motives, and behaviors in light of that.

2. If they (or God) find a problem, they will seek to make it right with God ASAP.

David explains in Psalm 51:16, 17: "Offerings and sacrifices are not what you want. The way to please you is to feel sorrow deep in our hearts. This is the kind of sacrifice you won't refuse." Remember, David wasn't asking forgiveness from God because he stole someone's iPod—he slept with someone else's wife, orchestrated a cover-up, and murdered her husband in the process! David was serious about asking for God's forgiveness and being sorry, aka repentant. God wants us to be deeply sorrowful when we injure Him with our sin. He wants more than words and actions; He wants the motivations of our hearts to be pure and right. He wants us to apologize for how we've injured our relationship with Him, not to be sorry just that we got busted.

A lot of people think that once God gave us salvation, then we got a "get out of jail free" card and we can live any way we want to. The apostle Paul corrects that idea in Romans 6:1, 2: "What should we say? Should we keep on sinning, so that God's wonderful kindness will show up even better? No, we should not! If we are dead to sin, how can we go on sinning?" If we're truly thankful for God's free gift of salvation, we won't live as close to the edge as we can, seeing absolutely how far we can go with sin or how much sin we can get away with. Instead, we'll stay as close to Christ as we can and not play games with sin.

Several weeks ago my wife told me about an interesting article she had read. It was about how people keep reptiles (cold-blooded animals) as pets, yet no matter how much somebody loves them, feeds them, and takes care of them, reptiles don't have the ability to form loving and caring bonds with their owners and can at any time turn on them—biting, hurting, injuring, and even killing them. It kind of brings a new understanding to the term "cold-blooded killer."

That's how dealing with sin is. No matter how much you play with it and spend time with it, in the end it still has no love or feelings for you and will ultimately kill you. With the text from Romans in mind, consider this: Are there things you've been thinking, watching, saying, or doing that you need to change? God loves you and doesn't want you living your life as if you don't know Him.

Jesus said plainly: "If you love me, you will do as I command" (John 14:15). Our love for God is most clearly and powerfully demonstrated by our obedience to Him. The church spends hundreds of thousands of dollars every year in creative programming, quality Bible teaching, and education that are second to none, and still many of our preteens, teens, and college students are apathetic, lazy, and mediocre Christians. They dress, talk, act, and look like the world.

I used to be one of those teens. I began doing my own thing in my mid-teens, and I didn't come back to God until my mid-20s. I wasted at least 10 of the most productive years of my life on my own sin and selfishness when I could have given them to God. Youth, don't be like me! The wise King Solomon, after having wasted a lot of his life, wrote these heavy words: "Keep your Creator in mind while you are young! In years to come, you will be burdened down with troubles and say, 'I don't enjoy life anymore'" (Ecclesiastes 12:1).

The reality is that if people don't see a positive difference in us as Christians, how will they ever want to choose Jesus over their sin and the world? The more sobering and scary thought is that some of those people may slip into eternity without ever knowing the hope, forgiveness, and peace that a relationship with Jesus can bring them, all because someone decided not to take seriously their relationship with Jesus and truly live as an "all-in" Christian.

So why do so-called Christians live like enemies of the cross of Christ (Paul's words in Philippians 3:17-19)? Simply because they don't truly love God. And they don't love God because they don't truly know God. I'm fully convinced that if they had a chance to really get to know God, they would love and trust Him, and if they truly loved and trusted Him, they would naturally want to do what pleases Him. After all, the Christian life is about living to please God, not ourselves. If you said you loved somebody and then lived any way you wanted to—totally disregarding what that person told you to do—how much would you truly love that person?

For some reason a lot of people think that God is this cosmic stick-in-the-mud. They think that all He's out to do is throw cold water on their fun. I've had teens say to me, "Omar, I want to follow God with all my heart, but if I do that, I can't have any fun!" And my response to them is "Sin isn't fun! The devil has got you fooled!"

Read Psalms, Proverbs, Ecclesiastes, or Romans, and you'll see a theme that repeats itself again and again: the only life, joy, freedom, health, and peace you're ever going to have is living a life that is within the borders of what God has prescribed! If you do what He doesn't want you to do, there's only sickness, selfishness, pain, and death. Oh, that you would hear what I'm saying to you and change your ways. Know God, respect and honor God, love and trust God, and finally obey God. He's your only hope!

What does it mean to truly obey and follow God? Jesus said to His followers—us included—"If any of you want to be my followers, you must forget about yourself. You must take up your cross each day and follow me" (Luke 9:23). Being a real Christian means that you don't put yourself first anymore; it means that you put Christ first. It means that you let go of your own interests and agenda. It also means that you've got to be willing to sacrifice for Jesus and deny yourself. It means that you've got to conform and submit to Him entirely and be willing to make changes in your life if Christ is telling you to do so. I hope we all want to be followers of Jesus. If that's the case, we have to be selfless, not selfish.

What does God want for us to give up, anyway? Only things that hurt our bodies, our minds, our characters, and ultimately our relationship with Him. It takes two hands and your whole body to carry a big, heavy, rough, wooden cross. Your mind and attention need to be focused on what you're doing. If you're doing it daily, you won't have time or motivation to focus on anything else but Jesus. When Jesus says "follow Me," that's a message of exclusion! You can't follow Jesus and something or somebody else. Your sole focus needs to be on Him. Think about where your focus is: are you following yourself, other stuff, the devil, or God?

The apostle John in four of his five books in the Bible (John and 1–3

John) keeps coming back to this central point: as Christians we ought to be known for our love. He then focuses on how this love should affect not only our relationship with God, but also our relationships with our Christian family and others. You might call him the "apostle of love." I know, I know, it sounds like some kind of cheesy radio or TV show host name. But all joking aside, why would a guy who spent so much time with Jesus spend so much time focusing on this issue?

Well, I've given it a lot of thought, and the only thing that I can think of is that John spent three years hanging out with Jesus, so he ended up becoming like Him and focusing on what Jesus wanted to focus on. In John 3:16, 17 John records Jesus' core mission statement: "God loved the people of this world so much that he gave his only Son, so that everyone who has faith in him will have eternal life and never really die. God did not send his Son into the world to condemn its people. He sent him to save them!" Did you catch it? Don't miss it. Jesus came to this world because God loved us so much that He couldn't bear to see any of us die, so Jesus sacrificed Himself for us.

I also think it's interesting that the night before He was crucified, Jesus brought together His disciples, and they spent special time having one last meal together. Before dinner was over, Jesus abruptly got up, washed everybody's feet (usually what a servant or slave would do), and then proceeded to drop a bomb on them. These words encompassed what He had been about since He was born, and they would continue to ring in John's ears until the day he died. Here's what Jesus said: "But I am giving you a new command. You must love each other, just as I have loved you. If you love each other, everyone will know that you are my disciples" (John 13:34, 35). Boom! Jesus basically said it's not what you say, it's what you do . . . and the kicker is that we should love each other as Jesus loved us. How did Jesus love us? Sacrificially!

John knew Jesus personally, and he made this incredible claim in 1 John 3:4-10 that everyone who loves and truly knows God will stop sinning, and if they don't stop sinning, then they don't know and love God. Whoa! Is this true? Well, let me explain. It's true that the Holy Spirit teaches us to say no to sin and strengthens and empowers us not to sin. But sin is deeply ingrained in our bodies and minds; that's why Jesus tells us that we have to die to sin and to our sinful nature (flesh).

There's no way that we can give our flesh a sensitivity course on the importance of sharing with others, being holy, and the like—it doesn't care!

It wants to do what it wants to do. Have you ever tried to reason with a newborn baby? When it's hungry, it's hungry—and it doesn't care if you're asleep.

John also says that you can distinguish the devil's children from God's children through two very important behavioral indicators: (1) they refuse to do right, and (2) they don't love each other.

John isn't talking about somebody who for the majority of their life is living a strong Christian life and has a slipup now and then. He's speaking about people who consistently and purposefully continue sinning—even when they know what is right. That's why he says those people "refuse to do right." They know better, but they don't do it.

Do you see a theme forming here? It's all about what you're doing, because what you're doing is an incredibly accurate indicator of what you're thinking and feeling. No matter where I go, I hear from teens, "C'mon, Omar, you can't just always lump people into one group or another based upon what they do, can you? Maybe they're just nice people, but you don't know them. You don't know the whole story!"

You know what I say? If a person put a gun to your head and robbed you, would you argue that the person was a nice person but just misunderstood? Would you argue that we can't figure out what kind of stuff they're thinking or feeling or what their true motivations are? Of course not! Why? Because you just got robbed at gunpoint—and they were at the safe end of the gun! That criminal's behavior made it crystal clear what they were thinking about, didn't it?

That's exactly the point that John is trying to make. He's saying that God's children truly have His Holy Spirit controlling them, and it changes them from the inside out. It's a pretty cool circular argument that makes sense. If you've been saved, then the Holy Spirit comes to live inside of you and you become a child of God. If you're struggling with sin but are making a genuine and concerted effort to fight your evil flesh, then the Holy Spirit stays to empower you to win the battle. As you win battle by battle, the Holy Spirit continues to clean you up from the inside out, and you continue not to sin and continue being a child of God. But if you consistently, continually, and blatantly sin—without conscience—then you are a child of the devil. Why? Because the Holy Spirit can't and won't live somewhere He's not wanted.

If you tell God that you're going to run the show, He's sad, but He leaves. Remember, you can't be filled with both yourself and God (the Holy

Spirit). It's either you or Him; someone's got to be in charge, and someone's got to go. So in light of all of that, I've got only one question for you: Whose child are you—God's or the devil's?

The truth is that becoming a Christian is the easiest thing in the world to do, but remaining a true Christian and staying saved is a more difficult work of a lifetime—but we can win the war against ourselves, sin, the devil, and the world. It will take constant surrender to God and the power of His Holy Spirit combined with our own will to do it, but it can be done. For if we are to win this world for Jesus, we've got no other choice than to work hand in hand with Him in order to get it done.

God's Word tells us very clearly in Galatians 6:7, 8 that there is a logical consequence for living your life outside of the bounds of what God has said is OK—and it is death.

The author of Hebrews paints a clear picture of what this type of "Christian" has to look forward to: "But what about people who turn away after they have already seen the light and have received the gift from heaven and have shared in the Holy Spirit? What about those who turn away after they have received the good message of God and the powers of the future world? There is no way to bring them back. What they are doing is the same as nailing the Son of God to a cross and insulting him in public!" (Hebrews 6:4-6).

This passage speaks about a Christian who isn't a "baby" in Jesus anymore—in other words, this person didn't just recently become a Christian. This person has had an increasing depth of knowledge and intimacy with God and has decided, "Nah, even though going with God is the way, I'm still going to do my own thing anyway." This passage is serious. It's important for somebody who is considering going their own way to think about this. Also, this passage is describing somebody who has once received salvation, but is not actively resisting the impulses and desires of their flesh (the evil inside of them) and who consistently and consciously chooses to sin.

Here's the bottom line: It's our decision to fall away from a relationship with Jesus and thereby lose our salvation. Our decision to fall away is not sealed with one sinful decision; it's sealed because of a lifestyle of consistent and purposeful sin and progressively worse and worse attitudes toward God. The further we get from God, the less and less we're able to hear His voice as He continues to call for us to come back home.

There will come a time that we will tell God by our attitudes and our behaviors that we don't want anything to do with Him, and we'll be excluding ourselves from heaven. If we're sinful and selfish, we would hate heaven. Heaven is a place of perfection and peace. In fact, for a sinful, selfish person, heaven would be hell!

God loves people too much to have them live in a place where they wouldn't be happy. These types of people would be miserable in heaven because everybody there is focused on God and on others, not on themselves.

Ellen White, in her classic book *Steps to Christ*, says this interesting thing about what would happen if sinners got to heaven: "The sinner could not be happy in God's presence; he would shrink from the companionship of holy beings. Could he be permitted to enter heaven, it would have no joy for him. The spirit of unselfish love that reigns there—every heart responding to the heart of Infinite Love—would touch no answering chord in his soul. His thoughts, his interests, his motives, would be alien to those that actuate the sinless dwellers there. He would be a discordant note in the melody of heaven. Heaven would be to him a place of torture; he would long to be hidden from Him who is its light, and the center of its joy. It is no arbitrary decree on the part of God that excludes the wicked from heaven; they are shut out by their own unfitness for its companionship. The glory of God would be to them a consuming fire. They would welcome destruction, that they might be hidden from the face of Him who died to redeem them" (pp. 17, 18).

When you sin willfully and purposefully, it's as if you spit in God's face. The Bible says that you insult God! Why do you insult God? Because you're basically saying that the life that His Son, Jesus, gave for you is really worthless. Again, that's pretty serious stuff! Let me ask you a question: Are you falling away? Have you fallen away? Here's a hint: If you're concerned about falling away, then you probably haven't done it. But have you been insulting God with the way you've been living your life? If you have, make changes right now. Don't wait another second.

The Bible tells us in Hebrews 10:26-29 what a purposeful sinner has to look forward to: hellfire and death—eternal separation from God. If we're striving to be genuine Christians, we shouldn't be sinning on purpose. When we have an unrepentant attitude, we reject and trample God under our feet, in effect treating God's sacrifice of His Son as an unholy or worthless thing. When somebody has reached this point in their spiritual walk and they don't turn back, there's only one place left to go—and it's not heaven. They wouldn't be happy anywhere else, actually.

When my children act like fools and become disrespectful or

consistently defiant, they typically receive discipline (a spanking) from me and are sent to their room for a period of time to "cool down." When I give them these consequences, they're usually really mad at me. But I find myself telling them more and more, "I love you, but don't get mad at me; you brought this down upon yourself through your behavior. Everything I do is in response to you."

God is our heavenly Father, and when we're consistently disobedient and defiant toward Him, He'll either give us discipline or step back and allow some very painful consequences to come our way. Why? Because we have free will, and God loves us too much to force us to do anything that we don't want to do.

When God doesn't apply His Son's salvation to our behalf, it's not because He doesn't want to; it's simply because He can't. We've made our choice through our bad behaviors and bad decisions. And after the consequences comes the "time-out," but unfortunately, this one isn't temporary, but eternal. Oh, how it will grieve the heart of God for ceaseless ages to have to give you your heart's desire and let you be destroyed by hellfire and eternally separated from the beautiful, eternal relationship that can be had with Him!

Why would any of us choose sin over God? If I'm speaking to you, then don't wait another second—get right with God and stay right with God. He'll give you the motivation and the power to do it. Hebrews 12:14 says: "Work at living in peace with everyone, and work at living a holy life, for those who are not holy will not see the Lord" (NLT).

God wants us to pull out all the stops and give it everything we've got! He wants us to take this holiness stuff seriously. God wouldn't ask us to be holy if He didn't give us the motivation, power, and focus to be able to do it. Let me ask you another question: Are you striving to be holy? If you are, are you trying to do it with or without God's power?

As Christians we are excited that Jesus died to give us salvation, but many times as we continue in our relationship with Him we can become complacent and lazy and forget that Jesus is not only our Savior but our Lord as well.

I know it's difficult reading some of this stuff, but I say it because I care and I want you to bear good—not rotten—fruit. The apostle Paul—who used to be a serious sinner, psycho, and murderer—wrote to the Christians in Corinth: "Anyone who belongs to Christ is a new person. The past is forgotten, and everything is new" (2 Corinthians 5:17).

Have you ever seen a butterfly chewing on leaves? Of course not! Why? Because butterflies don't eat leaves; they slurp on flower nectar. They're no longer caterpillars. When they were caterpillars, they dug leaves; they were also slow, fat, earthbound creatures, but now they are sleek, beautiful, heaven-bound butterflies. Butterflies don't eat the same stuff, they don't like the same stuff, they don't even look the same—they're totally different creatures.

When you became a Christian, everything about you changed! Everything became new! You're not the same person you used to be. Let me put it another way: *You don't have to be* the same person you used to be. Here's the real question: Can people tell that you're a Christian? I'm not talking about people you know; I'm talking about people you don't know. I mean, do you like the same sinful stuff you used to like before you were a Christian? Do you think the same, act the same, talk the same, watch the same stuff, listen to the same music, and dress the same (I'm talking about sinful, worldly things here)? I hope not. If you do, the Bible says that if you're consistently acting like a non-Christian, then you're not a Christian! I know it's pretty harsh, but true.

The apostle John wrote: "Don't love the world or anything that belongs to the world. If you love the world, you cannot love the Father" (1 John 2:15). We can't love both God and the world (the stuff that is opposed to God and His ways). We have to make a choice. Choosing to accept God is an either-or proposition. Either you choose God, or you choose the world; you can't choose both. Do you love God more, or do you love the world more? Would your friends and family agree with you? If you love the world more, what steps do you need to take to make a change toward God?

Jesus described the kind of relationship we should have with Him and with the world. Again, it's an either-or proposition. He said: "Go in through the narrow gate. The gate to destruction is wide, and the road that leads there is easy to follow. A lot of people go through that gate. But the gate to life is very narrow. The road that leads there is so hard to follow that only a few people find it" (Matthew 7:13, 14). We have read and heard this passage so many times, but we tend to overlook the fact that not only is the gate narrow, but the road is narrow as well.

You can't call yourself a Christian and live any way that you like. Remember, the old you is dead and your body is not your own, so honor God with the choices you make in life. Which gate and road are you taking? The easy, wide one, or the small, narrow one? If you're on the wrong road, remember that God accepts U-turns, but that means you've got to ask Him for forgiveness and turn—aka repent—from doing those things, saying those things, thinking those things, and watching those things. Tell Him you're sorry for crucifying Him all over again and ask Him to give you both the motivation and the power to do the things that make Him happy. I promise—you can have peace with Him today . . . right now. Don't wait another second!

I believe we're living in earth's very last days and Jesus is coming back soon. As Christians we need to be seriously focused on working for Jesus to complete His vision, mission, and goals, not our own. The only way that we can do this is if we're totally sold out to Him.

The temptations, impulses, and thoughts that you struggled with before will still be there after you accept Jesus, but now you've got a new weapon to deal with them. This is the same weapon that Jesus used very effectively and that enabled Him—as a human being (just like you and me)—to overcome His flesh nature, temptation, the world, and the devil. Do you know what weapon it was? It was a constant, daily, moment-by-moment relationship with, and total dependence on, God. That's how Jesus did it, and we can do it too!

While in prison the apostle Paul, probably in the second-to-last letter of his life, wrote to a young, introverted, unsure-of-himself pastor named Timothy. Paul boldly told him: "Don't let anyone make fun of you, just because you are young. Set an example for other followers by what you say and do, as well as by your love, faith, and purity" (1 Timothy 4:12).

Jesus is reminding you today that if this job of evangelism is to get done, it's going to start with you! You can set an example for other Christians. Don't let other people—no matter how old—look down on you and treat you with disrespect. God has saved you for a purpose and given you at least one spiritual gift. Use it for Him!

Jesus, immediately following the Last Supper, dropped a spiritual bomb on His disciples: "I tell you for certain that if you have faith in me, you will do the same things that I am doing. You will do even greater things" (John 14:12). This applies to not only them, but you as well! Jesus will give you the power to do even greater things than He did. God promises you the power to take the work of Jesus worldwide, to do big things for His kingdom. I hope that, given this information, you will be emboldened to give God and others your all.

Neither God nor I want you to live a mediocre Christian life. Listen to me: give God all of your life! Don't hold anything back from Him. Let the light of His love and holiness and the power of His Holy Spirit totally cleanse you from all sin. Sell out to God; you won't be sorry you did. True salvation must first begin with full conversion and be followed with daily sanctification. Then and only then are we guaranteed God, heaven, and glorification! But when we do, we'll want to tell everybody about the love, peace, forgiveness, and indescribable joy we have.

ROTTEN FRUIT MEANS ROTTEN ROOT

On the *Insight* Web site I came across this prayer request that is so real and so honest and so painful:

I ask that you would please pray for me. Lately I've been struggling with a number of things. I watch and read things that I know I shouldn't be watching or reading, and I find it hard to tear myself away from them. I use words/ language that I shouldn't be using. I have a problem with masturbation (for other girls who feel as though you're the only person that has problems with masturbation, you're not alone). My boyfriend and I have been struggling with being too touchy. We've both been Seventh-day Adventists since we were very small children. We know what's right and wrong; we're just finding it so difficult to have self-control. I'm yearning for a closer relationship with God. I hate feeling so far away from Him, feeling as if I'm drowning in all this sin. I just want an escape . . . and I'm just asking that you keep me in your prayers. I know that God hasn't given up on me, so I'm not giving up on Him. Thank you.—Struggling on the Inside.

Dear "Struggling,"

I'm glad you sent us this prayer request, and I believe that a lot of people—not just teens—feel this way a lot of the time.

The first thing I want to let you know is that I'm proud of your courage for choosing to step out of your comfort zone and write to us in such an honest manner. I also want you to know that God still loves you so very much, just as He always has. Even on your worst days of sinning, bad habits, self-hatred, guilt, shame, and all the bad stuff that goes with that, God still loves you. But it absolutely hurts Him that you're hurting.

As I read and reread your prayer request, I realized that I've felt this way before—and not just once. In fact, I was feeling this way just the other night. Let me tell you a little about my past and my present. I'm a recovering pornography (and all that goes with it) addict. I was involved in this sin, and it was like a boa constrictor. Any sin is, but especially sexual sin; it seems to promise so much: fun, freedom from self-control, love, intimacy, closeness, and acceptance. But little by little it squeezes, and squeezes, and squeezes you until it takes away everything from you, and it ultimately eats you alive . . . ewwww!

I know that you're struggling with other sins, too: the stuff you watch and read, and dirty language. But all this is only the fruit; what we need to talk about is where it all comes from: the root.

Let's look at what Jesus had to say about our hearts and our habits. In Matthew 15:18-20 we learn that Jesus said our words and the things we do make us unholy and sinful because they come out of our heart. Jesus also pointed out: "You can tell what a tree is like by the fruit it produces. You cannot pick figs or grapes from thornbushes. Good people do good things because of the good in their hearts. Bad people do bad things because of the evil in their hearts. Your words [and actions] show what is in your heart" (Luke 6:44, 45).

You see, even Jesus uses this example of the things we say and do as being the fruit that others can see, but our hearts, our attitudes toward God . . . there's the root! So how do we change our hearts? Well, we can't change our hearts, because we're born sinners, and without Jesus' intervention, we'll die sinners. But Jesus stepped in and died for us, taking our sin and giving us His perfection. All we have to do is choose to accept it and moment by moment continue choosing to live in it.

Accepting Jesus' salvation is easy to do, but the moment-by-moment continual choosing to live in it is definitely much harder. Why? Because we are naturally sinful! Look at what the apostle Paul has to say about it and tell me if he's not describing our letter writer's experience:

"We know that the Law is spiritual. But I am merely a human, and I have been sold as a slave to sin. In fact, I don't understand why I act the way I do. I don't do what I know is right. I do the things I hate. Although I don't do what I know is right, I agree that the Law is good. So I am not the one doing these evil things. The sin that lives in me is what does them.

"I know that my selfish desires won't let me do anything that is good. Even when I want to do right, I cannot. Instead of doing what I know is right, I do wrong. And so, if I don't do what I know is right, I am no longer the one doing these evil things. The sin that lives in me is what does them.

"The Law has shown me that something in me keeps me from doing what I know is right. With my whole heart I agree with the Law of God. But in every part of me I discover something fighting against my mind, and it makes me a prisoner of sin that controls everything I do. What a miserable person I am. Who will rescue me from this body that is doomed to die? Thank God! Jesus Christ will rescue me.

"So with my mind I serve the Law of God, although my selfish desires make me serve the law of sin" (Romans 7:14-25).

You see, Paul, one of the super-ninja Christians of all time, couldn't keep it all together. Did you hear his anger and frustration with himself? He realized that within himself there was a great war going on between his old sinful self and God's Holy Spirit. He realized that although he loved God with everything that was in him, he still was weak in himself because he was born a sinner. But here's the main difference: Although he was tempted by sin and a part of him was strongly drawn to sin, he didn't do it. Why? Because God's Holy Spirit gave him a different choice. He didn't have to sin; he was no longer a slave to it. Space doesn't allow me to include the entire chapter of Romans 8 (read it on your own), but here's the bottom line: The unsaved person has no choice but to follow their sinful nature and sin, but as Christians we have another choice. We can choose to make different decisions—decisions that don't lead to sin, decisions that honor God and make Him happy.

Aren't you glad that you don't have to continue in your sins? I know I am. God, through Jesus' sacrifice and the Holy Spirit's power, has set me free from the very same stuff you are struggling with—and He can do it for you, too. In fact, He's waiting for you to ask Him to do it for you.

Basically, without God we're sinful through and through—we sin because we're sinners; we can't help ourselves. But Jesus died to give us another choice. We may always be tempted to sin, but we don't have to give in and do it. That's the good news of salvation—no, that's great news!

Look at what the Bible says about people who consistently and knowingly sin versus those who accept God's help: "You cannot fool God, so don't make a fool of yourself! You will harvest what you plant. If you follow your selfish desires, you will harvest destruction, but if you follow the Spirit, you will harvest eternal life" (Galatians 6:7, 8).

Now I want to take a look at a guy named David in the Bible. Like you, “Struggling,” David decided to make a series of unwise choices that drove him deeper and deeper into negative consequences—consequences to himself, to others, and ultimately to God. Like you, he was raised the right way and had good biblical examples and teaching, but got involved in sexual sin. He decided to do some gardening but planted some bad seeds, which dropped roots; we can see the fruit that resulted.

It sounds as if you’ve been feeling this way too: anger, physical and emotional separation from others, guilty conscience, hopelessness, shame, addiction, anxiety, depression, discouragement, despair, suicidal thoughts, lack of respect for self, lack of trust toward God and others, lack of closeness and intimacy with God and others, outright break in a relationship with God—and these things kill a person’s witness for Christ. Most of these consequences are based on David’s own experiences as written about in Psalms 32 and 51. You should give them a read.

I don’t know about you, but as I look at this list of fruit, it seems that this stuff is all rotten! I don’t want any of it. So once you realize the depths that unconfessed, uncontrolled, and repetitive sin can take you, where do you go from there? I mean, what do you do? Well, the first thing is to decide whom you love more: yourself or God. As a counselor I always try to figure out why people do stuff. What are they hoping to get out of a behavior?

“Struggling,” here’s the bottom line: If you love God more than yourself—or more than your sin, for that matter—make the decision to stop sinful behavior. Tell God you’re sorry for what you’ve done (confession) and then make sure you stay stopped (repentance). Put into your life people whom you can talk to honestly about what you’re doing. Accept God’s forgiveness, and don’t believe the devil’s lies. Recognize that you’ve started several bad habits that have to be broken, but God has promised to give you the power to overcome any and all bad habits and sinful behaviors.

When you’ve made the decision to love God more than anything else and you stop your sinful behavior with God’s help, then the next time you look at the fruit in your life, you can say without a doubt that the fruit you’ve got is fresh, not foul—ripe, not rotten! God promises you in Galatians 5:16-25 that if you’re guided by God’s Holy Spirit, you’ll live to satisfy Him, but if you’re guided by yourself, bad things will always happen. Paul also reminds us that we are spiritually dead and have no choice but to live by God’s Holy Spirit.

Did you catch that? Paul uses an interesting word: “if.” In verse 16 he says: “If you are guided by the Spirit, you won’t obey your selfish desires.”

Then the verse goes on to state that if you are not guided by the Spirit, you will do all those nasty, sinful things—bad, stinky fruit. But the flip side of this promise is also true: if you are guided by the Spirit of God, you will have wonderful, beautiful, sweet-smelling fruit.

"Struggling," you've got it all backward—you're feeling guilty, angry, and frustrated because you're doing all those "bad fruit" behaviors, but you're continuing to sin. You can't have bad roots and expect good fruit! You've got to get rid of the bad roots and replace them with good roots, and then you'll naturally have good fruit.

The truth is that the moment you make the decision to stop purposely continuing in sin, you'll be fighting not only your old habits and history of being a sinner, but also the devil, the world, and possibly your friends whispering in your ear. But we have this promise: "God is the one who began this good work in you, and I am certain that he won't stop before it is complete on the day that Christ Jesus returns" (Philippians 1:6). Translation: If God started the process of your becoming more and more like Him, He won't leave you high and dry.

So, "Struggling," don't give up hope. Keep having faith in God, and don't let discouragement get the best of you.

MODERN WARFARE: GOD'S STYLE

It was the middle of the night, and I got up because our next-door neighbor's dog wouldn't stop barking. As I went into the foyer, I stepped on the most dangerous and diabolical thing ever known to man: the Lego brick. This "toy" (if you can call it that—I call it a tool of death and destruction) literally punctured the sensitive, soft part of the bottom of my foot that doesn't actually touch the ground. I think the foot doctor I had to see called it my arch (which isn't so swoopy lately, thanks to the aforementioned Lego).

Anyhow, this incident taught me two deep and never-to-be-forgotten lessons about the devil's schemes. Here's the first one: What looks harmless to us in the light can be deadly to us in the dark. The naughty thing that seems easy to refuse when you're spiritually full and things are going great may be the same thing that seems so overly tempting once you've gone without Bible study and prayer for a day or two and the pressures of life seem overwhelming.

Here's the second thing this experience taught me: While the light is on and my son is awake, he needs to pick up everything and clear the floor. In other words, during times of strength it's important for us to prepare for times of weakness. That means doing such things as memorizing scripture that's applicable to our own weaknesses and temptations and making sure we're being strengthened by daily connecting with God and godly people.

The Bible calls the devil many things, but none of them are good: liar and father of lies, dragon, serpent, thief, murderer, Beelzebub, Satan, Lucifer, lion, the enemy, the evil one, the deceiver, the accuser, the prince of darkness. In general, all of these names—except for Lucifer (his name before he became evil)—denote someone who is evil and does evil things.

What are the devil's strategies? Well, he likes to make us question God's goodness, God's plans, and God's motives. He likes to make us think that we know better than God. He would like to just kill us if God wouldn't stop him—yes, he's that evil! He also uses his angels that got kicked out of heaven (now his demons) to work miracles, fool us, and even make themselves out to be good angels. The devil uses all kinds of tricks to get us to stray from God. Here's the important thing: He knows you—what your specific weaknesses are, your personality and character, your likes and dislikes, your pet peeves and quirks. And he at this very moment is probably watching and studying you in order to trip you up, discourage you, and get you in his clutches.

The devil and his demons were thrown out of heaven during a civil war. When they were thrown out, God sent them to earth. God made the wise decision to put them out because of the lies and outright rebellion that the devil instigated. The Bible calls the devil the prince of the air and this world. The devil is powerful, but God is more powerful! Ultimately the devil is a dog on a leash and can do nothing without God giving him express permission to do it (see Job 1).

There are four things that I want you to know about God:

1. God is greater and stronger than the devil.
2. God already won when He gave His Son, Jesus, to die on the cross for us, and He will ultimately win the final battle.
3. God wants you to be victorious over the devil and his demons.
4. God will go with you, He will never leave you, and He will give you all the skills and weapons you need to win battles and the ultimate war against the devil.

Let's take another look at what the Bible has to say about the devil. This is especially significant to those of you who are seriously considering accepting Christ, who just became Christians, who just got baptized, or who are presently going through difficulties.

Before we look at a Bible passage, let me give you some background on what's happening. Jesus has just asked his first cousin, John the Baptist, to baptize him. The Bible says that he dunked Jesus in the Jordan River, and as Jesus came out of the water, God let everybody know that He was happy about the whole thing and approved of it and of Jesus. Now read what happened next in Matthew 4:1-11 and we'll review what we can learn from it all:

1. The Holy Spirit led Jesus into the desert so that the devil could test him. Why do you think that was? Simply put, God allows us to be tempted and to receive trials and difficulties in our lives to draw us closer to Him and to make us more like Him.
2. The devil knew the Bible. Hello! The devil is the ultimate psychologist. He's had millenniums to watch human beings, to learn about our behavior, and to figure out what makes us tick.
3. The devil took the Bible out of context and twisted it to make it say what he wanted.
4. The devil tempted Jesus with the same three temptations—pride, position, and possessions—that he tempted Eve with (for more information, look at Genesis 3). We all know how well that went for Eve—and consequently for you and me. The devil tried to do the same thing with Jesus, but Jesus made a different choice, a right choice.
5. Jesus successfully overcame the devil through the power of God and through His knowledge of Scripture. If perfect, sinless, Son-of-God Jesus had to know His Scripture to overcome the devil, then how much more do we need to be reading and studying our Bibles so we can be ready with the Sword of the Spirit to fight off the attacks of the devil?
6. The devil tempted Jesus when He was in His weakest physical and emotional state. The devil's not stupid. He knows exactly when and how to tempt you. He's just like the computer company Dell: he'll custom make one, just for you!
7. Once Jesus successfully overcame the devil, the devil left—but he came back. He's like the Energizer Bunny: he just keeps going,

and going, and going. You read about how he worked through the religious leaders of Jesus' day and how he even worked through one of Jesus' inner circle of 12 followers—Judas Iscariot! Again, the devil's not a quitter. He's not going to let you go without a fight!

8. After the devil left, angels came to attend Jesus. Remember, God will never leave you alone. You have the eternal, inexhaustible resources of God on your side. If it was you versus the devil, my money would be on the devil, but you and God make a majority. The Bible says if God is for us, who can be against us!

So how can we prepare ourselves to do battle with the devil, and how can we beat him? When it came to dealing with this battle between good and evil and being aware of what it took to be successful in the Christian life—and just to literally stay alive—the apostle Paul was an old pro. Near the end of one of his letters to the Christians in the city of Ephesus, Paul addressed this issue very clearly and comprehensively. Remember, the Christians were used to seeing Roman soldiers walking around dressed in their full battle armor and carrying their swords, spears, and shields. So he used this as an example of how we need to be prepared to meet the devil and his angels in this battle for our hearts, our minds, and our very lives.

Read about it in Ephesians 6:10-18. Now let's look at a couple of really crucial points that we need to take away from this passage:

1. It is God's strength that makes us strong. Don't think for one moment that you can battle the devil or his demons in your own strength.
2. We must put on *all* the armor that God gives so we can defend ourselves against the devil's tricks. By the way, all the devil has is *tricks;* the reason is that if he came at you directly, you would push him away, so he has to be sneaky, deceptive, and underhanded.
3. We're not ultimately fighting against humans, but against the devil and his demons. Now, it's true that many times we fight against flesh-and-blood beings; but many times they are influenced by the spirit of the devil and his demons—they might even be controlled directly through demon possession. Yikes! I hope you want to be possessed by the Holy Spirit, not the unholy one!
4. Paul tells us to "be ready!" He knew all too well that the "day of evil" and the battle that followed it was coming our way—and we could

either be ready and stand firm or not be ready and die (spiritually speaking).

5. Every piece of God's armor has a lesson that we can apply to our lives:
   a. **BELT: GOD'S TRUTH.** Belts were not meant for civilian use but were the mark of a soldier. The belt was commonly used to hold the soldier's sword and/or dagger. I find it interesting that the belt supported the sword in place and kept it ready for the soldier to fight with in case he needed it. God's truth is the only truth that we should be using to fight off the devil. It's the only truth that will work because it's truly true! Everything else is man's knowledge, philosophies, and lies.
   b. **ARMOR OR BREASTPLATE: GOD'S JUSTICE.** This armor appears to have been a purely Roman invention. The armor was made up of many pieces of laminated iron all bound together with leather straps and metal hooks, forming a very flexible and strong barrier for the soldier. The armor protected the soldier's chest and torso—where the majority of the vital organs are. We can lose an arm or a leg, but if we get injured in this part of our body, we're in bad shape. The understanding that God is ultimately in control of what happens in this world and will ultimately make all things right can really take a lot of pressure off of us to get angry for all the wrong reasons and want to get even. Our faith in God's sovereignty should inform our knowledge of where and when to use the knowledge of the Scriptures.
   c. **SHOES: YOUR DESIRE TO SPREAD THE GOSPEL.** Roman military sandals used iron hobnails as treads, a lot like the cleats of a modern-day football player's shoes. This footwear was basically made for any and every situation and allowed the Roman soldier to fight with total confidence in any battle condition. Our desire to spread the gospel should come from the total confidence that this is what God put us on this earth to do!
   d. **SHIELD: YOUR FAITH.** The faith that we have is not in ourselves, but in God. The shield was the main form of body protection of the Roman soldiers. It served the purpose of deflecting missiles targeted at them, as well as protecting them from the impact of handheld weapons wielded at them. The shield's large size allowed the soldiers to form a shield wall that could protect

them all during an advance. Not only can your faith protect you, but also your faith can bolster the faith of others and protect them as well.

e. **HELMET: GOD'S SAVING POWER OR GOD'S SALVATION.** I find it interesting that Paul tells us to wear on our head the knowledge and assurance that we have salvation. Our brains are in our head, and God knew that the devil would consistently try to put doubts in our minds about our salvation.

f. **SWORD: GOD'S HOLY BIBLE.** This is the only offensive weapon. Every other part of the armor is used to defend us, but the Bible is used to fight back against the devil. The original Greek word used to describe the Bible means literally the "saying" of the Bible—not the writing or the reading. This is just how Jesus, when tempted by the devil, drove him away. Reading and writing the Bible are important and really help us move the knowledge from short-term to long-term memory. But when we speak it out loud in a situation that is stressful and tempting, it's absolutely amazing the resolution and conviction that we begin to feel—and the Bible tells us that if we resist the devil, he leaves. No, he flees! That means he runs away really fast!

Paul also says to "never stop praying, especially for others." Isn't it interesting that Paul distinguishes praying "by the power of the Spirit" from praying within our own power? Again, we are told to "stay alert."

We've learned about the devil's plans and organization of his demons and how they can disrupt good things that are meant for us. We learned that although we are treated badly by the devil and the world, we still have God's Holy Spirit with us, and there is nothing that can or will happen to us that's bad enough to ever separate us from the love of God. We also learned that the devil doesn't play fair, he attacks us when we're at our weakest, and he knows Scripture, so we must know it better and always fight him in the power of the Holy Spirit. Last, we learned that we must always be on our guard and put on all the armor of God, and we should never stop praying with the power of the Holy Spirit.

I hope you realize how important it is to know your enemy, the devil, but more important, to know God: the One who can give you—and has already given you—the power and victory over Satan. Paul wrote (from jail, of all places): "God wiped out the charges that were against us for disobeying the Law of Moses. He took them away and nailed them to the cross. There Christ defeated all powers and forces [of Satan]. He let the whole world see them being led away as prisoners when he celebrated his victory" (Colossians 2:14, 15).

So remember, in the darkest part of your life, when you step on the proverbial Lego piece, never forget in the dark what God has told you in the light. Suit up and get ready for battle, because God has promised you that greater is He (God) that is in you than he (Satan) that is in the world.

GREAT IS THY FAITHFULNESS!

I love my house. It was built in 1900, and it's *old!* But it's got tons of character, and I love everything about it. We're located smack-dab on Main Street. There are many days when I sit on my front porch and watch the interesting cast of characters ride, run, walk, and drive by. Trust me, here in small-town Plainville, Georgia, the people are anything but plain.

We have two ginormous pecan trees that give us both shade and lots of pecans. And we also have squirrels and birds that absolutely adore the nuts and worms in my front yard. One day I watched the squirrels insanely gathering nuts and a robin grabbing up tons of worms.

As I watched them I realized something quite profound: These animals have food *every day*, but God isn't going to put it in their mouths for them while they sit in their nests. They have to get up and work for it. Every day they are required to do their part, and every day God is required to do His part. No matter what happens, rain or shine, those animals are in my front yard foraging for food—and they always find it.

In the Old Testament book of Lamentations the prophet Jeremiah expresses deep grief after witnessing the Babylonians totally wipe out Jerusalem. In Lamentations 3:14-30 he complains about being made fun of by everyone and being depressed, but in verses 21-25 he wisely says: "Then I remember something that fills me with hope. *The Lord's kindness never fails! If he had not been merciful, we would have been destroyed. The Lord can always be trusted to show mercy each morning. Deep in my heart I say, 'The Lord is all I need; I can depend on him!' The Lord is kind to everyone who trusts and obeys him.*"

Maybe you feel this way sometimes. I know I do. Life is hard, and being a teenager today is even harder. There's a lot of stuff that you have to deal with that's . . . well, hard. But isn't it awesome to know that God never fails? His kindness, mercy, compassion, and grace are new every morning. It's like every day God fills our souls with just enough of His Holy Spirit "gas" to give us the power to do what we need to do.

Are you questioning God today? Are you depressed, anxious, or worried about something in your life? Do you feel like Jeremiah did when he said that God had made him eat gravel or rubbed his face in the dirt?

Maybe some of you have earthly fathers whom you're not close to or who have abandoned you, but I promise that God will never leave you and will be with you until the end of the world (Matthew 28:20). God is never further than a prayer away. Sometimes the only way we'll ever be able to truly know the light of God's love is when we're in total darkness. I'm not being mean or wishing that you'll have bad times in your life, but I can speak from personal experience that if you're living in this world, bad times will come. The times I've felt God closest to me were the times I felt furthest away from everybody else.

My favorite hymn is "Great Is Thy Faithfulness." There have been entire days and nights when I would repeat the words to myself again and again—not because I didn't believe them, but because I needed to be reminded of them in the midst of the stuff I was going through. The words of the song bring tears to my eyes because I know they reflect the heart of a God whose heart hurts when we hurt and who wants nothing more than to prove to us that His faithfulness is indeed *great.*

THE SQUEAKY WHEEL GETS THE GREASE

The squeaky wheel gets the grease, Omar!" I heard my father chastise me.

I had had a problem with one of the wheels on my bike being wobbly, and I didn't know how to fix it. So like every prideful, self-sufficient little boy, I waited and worried and waited and worried . . . until the wheel became so wobbly and unbalanced that it was becoming dangerous for me to ride down the road.

Cue my father. When he saw the problem, he immediately called me over, put his big fatherly arm around me, looked me in the eye, and said in his most serious but loving tone, "Omar, why didn't you come to me with this earlier? Don't you know that your wheel could have come off, and you really could have been hurt? Remember, Omar, the squeaky wheel gets the grease!"

In other words, my father would have been more than happy to solve my problem had I only had faith in him and come to him and not tried to solve it by myself. Thanks, Dad—lesson learned.

Fast-forward many years. Several weeks ago my wife woke me up about 5:15 in the morning and frantically said, "I'm sorry to wake you, but I think there's a snake in the living room fireplace!"

Now, I'm a father of two kids, and their room is right off the living room. So you can bet I didn't go back to sleep. I addressed the problem right away. I got up with my trusty stick, and sure enough, in the living room fireplace there was a loud hissing sound followed by what sounded like a lot of teeny little beeping fire alarms. Well, I did what any red-blooded American father would have done to protect his family: I pushed something large up against the fireplace door and told my wife to call "pest removal people."

I'm glad my smart wife didn't listen to me, but instead recorded the sound and immediately began doing Internet research. What she found was very interesting: we had a family of birds called chimney swifts living in our chimney. She gladly informed me that as loud as they were—and they were loud—they would likely be gone within the next two weeks. I was absolutely amazed at the sounds that came from the chimney and fireplace. Apparently our chimney acted like a great big amplifier, and the fireplace was like the speaker.

For the next two weeks or so, my family got to experience the wonder of hearing a parent bird fly down into the chimney. The moment that happened, all the baby birds would start their racket! As soon as they'd been fed, they stopped making sounds. Every once in a while a baby bird would fall out of the nest, and we would hear it flopping and flapping about. Then, within one to two seconds, would come the fervent shrill of its chirping, letting the parent know it needed help. Immediately we would hear the parent swoop in—literally—to save the day.

That experience got me to thinking about this: If babies and animals understand and obey this principle of the squeaky wheel, why do we as humans have such a hard time with it? Are we such stubborn knuckleheads that we have to wait until our "wheels come off" and we hurt ourselves until we call on God?

Well, lucky for us, God has yet again provided an interesting story for us to learn from. The story in Matthew 20:29-34 teaches an important lesson in making sure you get listened to—at any cost. It's the account of Jesus healing two blind men. There were three things that the blind men did right:

1. They knew that they were blind and that they needed to be healed. You might think, *Well, of course they knew they were blind.* But there are many people today who don't know they're spiritually blind. A lot of people think they're just fine. In fact, Jesus called many of the religious leaders of His day "blind guides" (see Matthew 23:16). I hope you're not one of those people. The Bible tells us that "all of us have sinned and fallen short of God's glory" (Romans 3:23).
2. They came to the only source they knew could heal their blindness. They didn't call after the disciples that were following Jesus or even the religious leaders who were likely listening to Jesus' teaching. No, they called out to Jesus. In another instance, after a great number of Jesus' disciples deserted Him after He was honest about the trials and difficulties that they would face, Jesus turned to his core group of 12 disciples and asked them if they were going to leave as well. "Simon Peter answered, 'Lord, there is no one else that we can go to! Your words give eternal life. We have faith in you, and we are sure that you are God's Holy One'" (John 6:68, 69). Where are you going to get your healing? in a relationship? in food, porn, stuff, drugs? There's only one source to get the healing you need, and that's Jesus.
3. The two blind men began to shout even louder when the crowd told them to be quiet. They were going to be sure that they got Jesus' attention. They wanted to be the squeaky wheels, and it worked. Jesus healed them. They didn't allow anyone or anything to take their focus off of getting healed. Many times our busy lives, our friends, our family, the devil, and even total strangers can take our focus off of following after Jesus. We must persist and stay focused on Jesus—and Jesus Himself said that we can be focused on only one thing.

I remember an old Japanese proverb my karate teacher used to tell me: "The eagle that focuses on the rabbit and the squirrel catches neither." Usually this was followed by some sort of painful blow to the body—because I wasn't focusing. Jesus had the same idea when He said: "If any of you want to be my followers, you must forget about yourself. You must take up your cross each day and follow me" (Luke 9:23). To follow Jesus, we must deny everything that takes our focus off of Jesus.

I hope that today you learned an important lesson in coming first to Jesus with whatever your problems are. No problem is too big and no problem is too small for Jesus.

BE GOD'S BALLOON

Recently my children went to a party that had a clown doing balloon art. Now, I'm sure that no one can go to college and take classes in balloon art, but this guy had everybody—even the adults—mesmerized with the different things he could make with just balloons. As I watched this clown do his thing, I realized that the magic wasn't found just in what he made, but also in the skill he showed making it. I also realized that the clown really, really loved bringing joy to the group.

After the cake came out, the song was sung, the candles were blown out, and the hungry hordes were chowing down, I cornered the clown and asked him some questions. I learned some interesting things. First, I was wrong: he did in fact attend clown college in Sarasota, Florida. He has a degree in "clown arts" from Ringling Brothers and Barnum and Bailey (the famous circus people). Second, I learned that he can use a balloon to make almost anything that people request.

The only thing that slows him down is "difficult balloons that are stiff, not stretchy, and are resistant to letting you work with them." I asked him what he does when this happens. He quickly responded, "Well, sometimes I have to stretch them, twist them, and wad them up to get them to be more manageable. It may take awhile, but I always get the balloon to cooperate. After all, these balloons all have different sizes, shapes, and colors, but this is what they were made for." I thanked him for his time (OK, I also put some money in his clown hat). After all, a clown shared deep, life-changing wisdom with me.

No matter what size, shape, and color we are, we're each made for a specific purpose: to glorify God through our lives. There's nothing particularly special about us, but the One who uses us to reach others is very special. Initially we may be resistant to God. When that happens, He has to stretch us, twist us, and sometimes wad us up to get us to cooperate, but in the end He'll do what it takes to get the job done. God loves, loves, loves to see people get saved. He is willing to use us as His balloons filled with the air of His Holy Spirit and shaped and twisted and molded to fit the unique and varied needs and requests of others. He'll do whatever it takes to reach others—and we are the tools He uses.

The prophet Jeremiah—depressed, fearful, and anxious about the people's negative and sometimes violent response to his ministry—pleaded to God, and God responded. Read what He said. It's found in Jeremiah 18:2-11.

God is the potter and we are the clay. Helping other people and being the "Jesus in their life" isn't always easy, and the responses we'll get won't always be positive. But what's the alternative? We turn our backs on God and the world and let everybody go to hell? Thank goodness that's not what Jesus did for us.

The apostle Paul had it right when he reminded the Corinthian believers that we should do whatever we can—taking on whatever shape we need to, so to speak—in order to share the gospel with as many people as we can (see 1 Corinthians 9:19-23).

We need to recognize that without Jesus' sacrifice of coming to this earth and becoming like one of us to reach us, we would be eternally lost (see John 1:14). Then we'll want to be Jesus' representatives on this earth to bring others to Him and to glorify Him. We'll want to let God use us and form and fashion us into whatever shape He wants in order to save as many of His children as He can. I don't know about you, but I want to be God's balloon and be filled with His hot air, rather than my own. I hope that today you'll decide to do the same.

I LIKE THE SMELL OF CLEAN

My wife recently bought the most wonderful product. I was absolutely enthralled by the name: "Miracle Cleaning Eraser." That's a big claim to make. On the package it says: "Cleans Just About Anything" and "Removes Scuffs and Soap Scum." It's a much cheaper knockoff of the Mr. Clean Magic Eraser, and the most interesting thing is that for being a "miracle," it comes in a plain white box.

One day my wife and daughter were using this product to clean tough, nasty stains off of our old claw-foot bathtub. These stains were the careful work of my 6-year-old son and his ongoing "experiments" with God's nature. Let me tell you: this product really works! But my wife and daughter wanted the bathroom to not just be clean, but smell "nice." So they also sprayed it with some awesome odor eliminator that had a fancy-sounding name like "Himalayan Mountain Unicorn Breath."

Immediately afterward, in stomped my son, sensing a disturbance in "the force." He smelled like a wet goat, with his rubber rain boots on and trees growing under his fingernails. He looked at them, looked at me, and inhaled deeply. Then he said one of the deepest spiritual things anybody has ever said: "Ahhhhh, I like the smell of clean!"

Of course he was talking about the smell of the recently sprayed bathroom, which he totally destroyed shortly thereafter. But his statement got me to thinking about my spiritual life—and yours. Each of us is blessed that we can come to Jesus, who is like that incredible little plainly packaged Miracle Cleaning Eraser. We can confess our sin, repent, and have that sin totally erased from our dirty, evil, selfish selves. The Bible promises: "If we confess our sins to God, he can always be trusted to forgive us and take our sins away" (1 John 1:9). "I, the Lord, invite you to come and talk it over. Your sins are scarlet red, but they will be whiter than snow or wool" (Isaiah 1:18).

But once we get clean, how do we *stay* clean? Well, the Bible covers that as well. It's found in John 15:1-7. I know that my elevator doesn't always go to the top, but even I can't miss the main point of what Jesus was trying to say: To have a healthy and intimate relationship with God—to stay clean—we've got to *be* and *stay* connected to Him. In this passage Jesus uses the phrases "stay connected to" or "stay joined to" eight times. So I have two questions for you: Have you ever been connected to Jesus? Have you ever accepted Him as your Lord and Savior?

It's simple to do. I recently heard a preacher say, "You can't *remain* where you've never *been*." Once you've gotten connected, just stay there. No matter what kind of good or bad things happen to you, stay connected to Him—not to other people or to stuff, but to Him. Many of the things that we're connected to aren't bad, but they're not Jesus. They can't give us eternal life. Only Jesus can make that claim.

The 12 disciples spent three years being with Jesus. They woke up with Him; they ate with Him; they watched Him teach, preach, heal, love on people, and challenge them too. During the day I'm sure they left His side for a while to pick up food or visit somebody who was sick or go somewhere and preach, but at the end of the day they always came back. They always ended their day connecting back with Jesus.

And so it should be with you. During the day, no matter what you do, whom you're with, or where you go, come back and connect with Jesus. When you succeed, and especially when you fail, come back to Jesus at the end of the day. Spend some time talking to Him about what your day was like. Connect with Him, and let that connection magically and powerfully erase all the grime and dirt and sin of the day. If you do this every day, day in and day out, I promise that you'll like the smell of clean.

YOU'RE DIRTY!

When I was a kid I loved to watch the *Peanuts* specials on TV. I loved how they would characterize adults as faceless, incoherent people. I also loved how I could identify with many of the experiences the characters were going through. But the thing I loved the most was how every character matched at least one person I knew.

Do you remember the character named Pig-Pen? He was filthy and dirty, and everywhere he went a cloud of dust and dirt surrounded him. The crazy thing was that he acted as though he didn't even know . . . or care!

Well, the Bible tells us that if we're not careful, we can end up in the same boat—spiritually speaking. Revelation, the last book of the Bible, opens with letters of warning to several churches. Check out Revelation 3:14-20 to read God's message to Laodicea.

Wow! God is disgusted and offended with these people. What did they do to cause Him to respond in such a strong fashion? Here's the bottom line: They had forgotten their real need for Jesus. They thought they had all they needed in life—money and success—but in reality, without a relationship with Jesus, none of it mattered. Jesus Himself said: "What will you gain, if you own the whole world but destroy yourself? What would you give to get back your soul?" (Matthew 16:26).

These people thought they had it all together, but they, like Pig-Pen, didn't realize that they were "pitiful, poor, blind, and naked" (Revelation 3:17). Could it be that God is so disgusted with us for the same reason?

Could it be that we're so consumed by foolish pride and selfish desires (1 John 2:16) that we barely hear Jesus knocking on the doors of our hearts? Where do you think that leaves Him when we have an "I got this" attitude? It leaves Him on the outside.

So how do we fix the problem? How do we get Jesus from the outside to the inside? First we must recognize that we're all sinful and that we all need God's forgiveness and salvation. Jesus said it best when He told the crowds: "God blesses those people who depend only on him. They belong to the kingdom of heaven!" (Matthew 5:3). God wants us to recognize our total emptiness of anything good or worthy that we can bring to Him. We must realize that the only thing that will satisfy the God-thirst in our lives is God. King David wrote: "As a deer gets thirsty for streams of water, I truly am thirsty for you, my God. In my heart, I am thirsty for you, the living God. When will I see your face?" (Psalm 42:1, 2). Do you hear his focus to get to God . . . and not other things?

God tells us that the only cure for our "Pig-Pen-ness" is Him. So He calls us to take from Him the true riches of fellowship with Him: the covering of His righteousness and His wisdom to rightly see our lives from His point of view. Once we do that, we'll willingly open the door of our hearts to Him so He can come in, have a real relationship with us, and clean us up from the inside out.

When this happens, not only will God stop being disgusted with us, but we'll want to share what we've found with everyone we meet. In the final lines of the last book of the Bible, there are two appeals; God makes the first one: "If you are thirsty, come! If you want life-giving water, come and take it. It's free!" (Revelation 22:17). The second one is a natural consequence of our close relationship with God. The apostle John, also known as "the disciple whom Jesus loved," tells us his heart cry: "So, Lord Jesus, please come soon!" (Revelation 22:20).

LIGHT'S OUT?

Several weeks ago two telephone poles—with their telephone and electric lines—got violently ripped out of the ground by the garbage truck. It caused wreckage and chaos all over our road and knocked out our phones and Internet for several days.

As I watched the different companies come out and reestablish our services, I quickly realized that this accident had also knocked out several streetlights. Now, we have beautiful black turn-of-the-century reproduction streetlights that look like they're made of cast iron with fancy scrollwork on the pole and the top. Everybody who comes to visit us mentions how pretty they are. The city must have paid a lot of money for each one.

After I called and reported the issue, all the streetlights were quickly fixed . . . except for one: the one on the corner of an intersection of two streets right beside my house. Now, that might not seem important, but a lot of stuff goes down on those two particular streets. Out of all the spots in the streets of Plainville, this spot needs the most light!

It's amazing how something isn't noticed until it's not working. I mean, the whole street was brightly lit . . . all except for that one spot. As I sat on my front porch listening to the sounds of the night and wondering what kinds of naughty naughtiness were being planned for the night's "fun," I got to thinking how things might be different if that streetlight was on, awake, aware, and doing its job.

Fast-forward several days. The wonderful folks with Georgia Power came out, unscrewed the lamppost, took it apart, inspected it, found the problem, and fixed it. Now we have consistent, *safe* lighting all night long.

Watching all that drama got me thinking about our role as lights shining for God in a dark and dreary world. Jesus tells us that as Christians we're to shine for God so others can see and praise Him (Matthew 5:15, 16). He also tells us through the apostle Paul that Christians should "be the pure and innocent children of God. You live among people who are crooked and evil, but you must not do anything that they can say is wrong. Try to shine as lights among the people of this world, as you hold firmly to the message that gives life" (Philippians 2:15, 16).

Jesus makes it clear that our role in this world is to shine for Him, but what happens when we stop shining? As far as streetlights go, the ones we have in our town look breathtakingly beautiful. But up until a few days ago, a strategically placed one didn't work. So I ask: What good is a streetlight if it doesn't work? What happens to it?

Well, believe it or not, there's a story in the Bible about this issue. It has to do with one of the early churches in the important city of Ephesus. This church had it all together—at least when they got started. They were on-target and shining brightly for Jesus, but then life happened, and the individual and collective lights began to burn less brightly, and then they went out altogether. How sad. They were like that streetlight in my neighborhood that just looked pretty but didn't work.

Listen to the warning God gave this church:

"This is what you must write to the angel of the church in Ephesus:

"I am the one who holds the seven stars in my right hand, and I walk among the seven gold lampstands. Listen to what I say.

"I know everything you have done, including your hard work and how you have endured. I know you won't put up with anyone who is evil. When some people pretended to be apostles, you tested them and found out that they were liars. You have endured and gone through hard times because of me, and you have not given up.

"But I do have something against you! And it is this: You don't have as much love as you used to. Think about where you have fallen from, and then turn back and do as you did at first. If you don't turn back, I will come and take away your lampstand. . . .

"If you have ears, listen to what the Spirit says to the churches. I will let everyone who wins the victory eat from the life-giving tree in God's wonderful garden" (Revelation 2:1-7).

Ephesus was a center of land and sea trade, and along with Alexandria and Antioch in Syria, it was one of the three most influential cities in the eastern part of the Roman Empire. The Temple of Artemis, one of the ancient wonders of the world, was located in this city, and a major industry was the manufacturing of images of this goddess.

The church at Ephesus had become a large, proud church. They were proud of their accomplishments both in and out of the church. The Ephesians had bragging rights: Paul ministered in Ephesus for three years, which would seem to indicate that the work there was especially fruitful. Paul spent more time at this church than at any other place on his recorded missionary journeys. Christianity appears to have been preached there first by Paul. At the time that the book of Revelation was written, Ephesus must have been one of the leading centers of Christianity.

Yet Jesus spoke to this church first, not because of its size or the number of members or the wonderful needs-based outreach ministries that they were doing. No! Jesus addressed this church first because of the seriousness of the sin that they were committing. Jesus' message had to get their attention, and it did. He had to remind them of right and proper priorities—of what was really important! Deeds are not going to get us to heaven—a relationship with Jesus is. The problem is that many of us have religion without relationship. The secret is relationship, not religion.

We see in Revelation 2:1-7 the keys to regaining an intimate relationship with God. I call them the four R's:

- Recognize the problem.
- Remember the relationship.
- Repent of our sins.
- Reprioritize our lives accordingly.

Let me give you two pieces of background on this passage:

1. Jesus Himself gave the words to John (Revelation 1:12-18). Jesus cared about what the churches and individuals were going through, and He still cares. Jesus is a personal God.
2. The seven lampstands mentioned in this passage are the seven churches (Revelation 1:20). All of these churches had a very important part to play in the life of both Christians and non-Christians all over the world.

Now let's move on with our examination of the passage in Revelation 2. The first thing you must do in order to keep a vibrant and intimate relationship with God is to recognize the problem (verses 1, 2). God says: "I know your deeds" (verse 2, NIV). You can never hide the truth from God. He knows why you're doing the things you're doing. The church in Ephesus didn't have a problem with their deeds, but they had lost their focus of what was most important. Their motivation wasn't right. Where has your focus shifted? Are you too busy doing "good" things for God and not taking enough time to connect with Him daily?

The next thing you must do to ensure that you have a vibrant relationship with God is to remember the relationship. Verses 4 and 5 say: "You have forsaken the love you had at first. Consider how far you have fallen!" (NIV). "Forsaken" in the original Greek language of the Bible means "deserted, abandoned, to have divorced." Can you imagine getting to a place in your relationship with God that it seems like you divorced Him? Many of you come from families that have been ripped apart by divorce. When God uses this term, it's not good.

The word "first" is translated in the original Greek as "before," or "most important." The word "love" in the original Greek is the word *agape*. That's the kind of selfless and totally sacrificial love that Jesus had for us that drove Him to die on the cross for us. That's the kind of love that we should have for Him—and for others! The word "fallen" in the original Greek literally means "failed" or "to die." I don't know about you, but I don't want my relationship with God to die! And if it's dead, I want God to bring it back to life.

We must have daily communion and communication with God to keep a vibrant and intimate love relationship with Him. Are reading/studying the Bible and praying a bore to you? Then ask God to give you the strength and excitement again. David stated: "Create in me a pure heart, O God, and renew a steadfast spirit within me. Do not cast me from your presence or take your Holy Spirit from me. Restore to me the joy of your salvation and grant me a willing spirit, to sustain me" (Psalm 51:10-12, NIV).

The next step we must do to revive our relationship with God is to repent of our sins. Revelation 1:5 warns: "Repent and do the things you did at first" (NIV). Once you ask God for forgiveness, you've got to start doing something different from what you did before. The only way you or I can be saved is by faith, and faith is trust. You can't trust someone you don't know. What's the only other option? Verse 5 continues: "If you do not repent, I will come to you and remove your lampstand from its place" (NIV). The word "remove" in Greek means "disgrace, scorn, insult, offensive."

In other words, if the church didn't make a radical change, it would forfeit its status as a *real* representative of Christ. Revelation 1:20 tells us that the lampstand represents the church, but Zechariah 4:2-6 and Revelation 4:5 make it clear that the oil that makes that lamp burn symbolizes the Holy Spirit. Don't miss it: the church—and the person—would continue to exist, but the power that made it distinct and effective would be missing!

Now, how does that apply to you and me? Are we just going through the motions? For Jesus to "remove your lampstand from its place" would mean that the church would cease to be an effective representative of Christ. Just as the seven-branched candlestick in the Temple gave light for the priests to see, the churches were to give light to their surrounding communities. But Jesus warned them that their lights could go out. In fact, Jesus Himself would remove any lamp or candle that had been extinguished. The church as a whole had to repent of its sins.

The last thing we must do to revive our relationship with God is to reprioritize our lives accordingly (Revelation 2:7). There's no point in hearing the Word of God if you're not going to do something about it. This passage implies that those who hear will do so *with understanding and action*. Hearing God's Word is meaningless unless the life is not immediately changed to the pattern of what has been heard.

Just as when a guy and girl fall in love, so also new believers rejoice at their newfound forgiveness. But when we lose sight of our relationship with Jesus, we lose sight of the seriousness of sin and the separation it causes. Then we begin to lose the thrill of our forgiveness.

In the first steps of your Christian life, you may have had enthusiasm without knowledge. Do you now have knowledge without enthusiasm? Both are necessary if we are to keep love for God intense and pure. We must have continual daily communication and communion with God to keep a vibrant and intimate love relationship with Him. If we don't, we'll stop being a light in a dark world. Instead, we'll be a candle with no light, a streetlight that doesn't work—good for nothing! We'll stop being part of the solution and become part of the problem. Let me ask you a question: Do you love Jesus with the same power and passion as when you were a new Christian? What did you do differently then that you're not doing now?

As we have seen, the Ephesians needed a wake-up call. They thought they could coast into heaven on their works—their religion—instead of their relationship. But God required of them something deeper, something more: an intimate, daily love relationship with Him. He needed them to have a relationship, not religion. He asks nothing less than that of you and me. So I have one final question for you today: Is your light out? If it is, do something, and do it quickly, because if you don't, Jesus will.

IT'S RAINING CATS AND DOGS!

Ah, summertime in Georgia . . . By my estimation there should be absolutely no sinners left in the state after they get a mild taste of what hell will be like. Wow, it's hot! I'm talking about sweating-while-you're-toweling-off-right-after-a-shower hot.

But for the past three days, God has mercifully been giving us a reprieve from the hellish heat by sending wind and rain. Of course, these freakishly heavy rain showers are the direct result of incredibly heavy rainfall from Florida all the way to Mississippi, causing riptides, flash floods, and other devastating problems. Come to think about it, maybe it's not God who's been sending these things our way.

While I write this I'm sitting in my living room, and it sounds as if there's a square-dancing hoedown happening on the roof of my home. I'm afraid the roof might fall in. It's raining cats and dogs!

My poor beat-down flowers are probably screaming in their teeny, weak, high-pitched, rain-soaked voices: "Enough, enough! Make it stop! We promise not to attack you with any more pollen!"

But all this rain has got me thinking about . . . well, rain. Especially what the Bible refers to as the latter rain. It's exciting stuff, and you and I can be a part of it—if we want to. What is the latter rain? What does it have to do with you and me, and how can we be a part of it?

Actually, before we can talk about the latter rain, we've got to talk about the former rain, or the rain that's already happened. When I talk about rain, I'm not talking about actual physical rain, but what the Bible refers to as the outpouring of God's Holy Spirit. You see, in the book of Acts, Luke records this about Jesus: "Before he was taken up, he gave orders to the apostles he had chosen with the help of the Holy Spirit. For forty days after Jesus had suffered and died, he proved in many ways that he had been raised from death. He appeared to his apostles and spoke to them about God's kingdom. While he was still with them, he said: Don't leave Jerusalem yet. Wait here for the Father to give you the Holy Spirit, just as I told you he has promised to do. John baptized with water, but in a few days you will be baptized with the Holy Spirit" (Acts 1:2-5).

Jesus promised the disciples that they would receive power to do the assignment He had given them, which was to share with the entire world the good news of salvation (Matthew 28:18-20). They didn't have to wait long, because in Acts 2:1-4 we read: "On the day of Pentecost all the Lord's followers were together in one place. Suddenly there was a noise from heaven like the sound of a mighty wind! It filled the house where they were meeting. Then they saw what looked like fiery tongues moving in all directions, and a tongue came and settled on each person there. The Holy Spirit took control of everyone."

In essence, through the Holy Spirit Jesus gave the disciples everything they would need to get the job done, and boy, did they need it! The Holy Spirit allowed them to speak and understand languages they didn't know; it gave them the power to raise the dead, heal people, get rid of demons, resist the venom of deadly animals, and so much more. Basically, Jesus, through the Holy Spirit, gave the disciples the power to complete the work that He started.

When you read the book of Acts, you see an incredible, interesting, true, and accurate account of what happened (the author was a doctor, after all). But the disciples didn't finish their job. We can be sure that they didn't finish their job because we're all still on this sinful earth and not in heaven with Jesus! Jesus told His disciples: "The Good News about the Kingdom will be preached throughout the whole world, so that all nations will hear it; and then the end will come" (Matthew 24:14, NLT).

You see, if you continue reading the account of the former or first rain of the Holy Spirit, you'll find the answer to the second or latter rain of the Holy Spirit. And here's an important fact: After this portion of the Holy Spirit, there won't be another.

Let's return to the story. The disciples were all hanging out in one room, and the Holy Spirit was given to them so powerfully that they all began speaking languages that they didn't know but that others understood. It was like 9:00 in the morning, and bystanders who didn't speak those specific languages thought that the disciples were drunk!

Peter cleared things up by explaining that they were witnessing the raining down of the Holy Spirit. He went on to speak the words of Joel, an Old Testament prophet: "When the last days come, I will give my Spirit to everyone. Your sons and daughters will prophesy. Your young men will see visions, and your old men will have dreams. In those days I will give my Spirit to my servants, both men and women, and they will prophesy" (Acts 2:17, 18).

Did you catch the importance of what Peter said? You and I are now the disciples who are in charge of completing the work that Jesus and His disciples began! All we need are a heart and spirit that are available and teachable—and the power of God's Holy Spirit (the latter rain).

Isn't that exciting? I truly believe that right now God has already started pouring out His latter rain. Do you want it? I know I do. It's absolutely mind-blowing to think that you and I could be alive to see Jesus coming in the clouds to take us all home! But that means that we've all got important work to do.

So do you know what specific "visions" has God given you to finish His work? What types of things are you naturally good at? Has God given you something to do that seems absolutely crazy, and you're kind of embarrassed to even mention it out loud because it seems so absolutely impossible?

Are you afraid that you could never do it on your own? Well, you can't. It requires God's Holy Spirit, and chances are good that it was God who gave that idea to you, so pray, pray, and then pray some more, but at the same time, talk to people. Get their wise advice, don't be discouraged or unfocused, and move forward in faith that God will continue giving you His Holy Spirit to get the job done that He started more than 2,000 years ago. God can and will use you—you've just got to ask for it to keep raining cats and dogs!

THE PROBLEM OF PAIN

He sat in front of me blankly staring out the window, expressionless, lost in his own world. He was 17 and had come to me for counseling. "Hey," I said, "what's going on with you today? It's like you're not even in this room."

He responded with frustration and anger. "I went to church last week with my mom just to get her off my back. It was boring! Man, church don't *ever* do nothin' to help me!"

I asked him another question: "If you could learn about anything at all—if you could have one burning question answered—what would it be?"

In a second he turned his entire body to face me. Then, staring me down like a pit bull eyeballing a steak, he softly said, "I'd wanna know: why do bad things happen to good people? I mean, if God is so 'good' and 'loving,' why did He take my grandmama away? Why did He let my mama do me like that? Why ain't my daddy around? Huh? *Huh?*" His eyes were locked onto mine, hoping for an answer. After realizing that I had nothing to say, he broke eye contact and slammed his fists down on the table, almost breaking it.

I was totally caught off guard by his show of raw emotion and his direct questions. I knew what he was referring to—though he *never* talked about it. For months I'd been trying to reach this kid, but for some reason at this moment the walls of his emotional dam broke, and all his hurt and pain came flooding forth in one overwhelming tsunami. This was the core of why he was so depressed, full of rage, and violent.

His question is an honest and real one: If God is loving, why is there so much evil and pain in the world? This kid didn't deserve any of this. He didn't ask to be born into a family with parents who abandoned him. All he had was his grandmother, and she was taken away. And now that he was finally connecting with his mother, she had gotten seriously ill. Why? This problem of pain is something that's universal to humanity. People get sick, divorced, and hurt. There's abuse, suicide, murder, war, misery, and pain. If God is so good, why is life so hard?

Well, God has answered this question for us through the biblical book of Job. It's an incredible true story of a man named Job who was holy, righteous, rich, and powerful. He had a prosperous business, a wonderful family, and a good life . . . until Satan got ahold of him.

Satan basically challenged God and told Him that the only reason Job was faithful was because God did good things for him. If God would allow Satan to destroy Job's life, he would curse God and turn his back on his Lord. Initially, one might think that Satan was trying to test Job's goodness, righteousness, and faithfulness, but actually this was a test of God's goodness, faithfulness, and love. You see, Job's story is just a small example of a larger fight that Satan has with God. And the entire universe is watching how it all plays out on Planet Earth. Unfortunately, Job—like us humans—was caught smack-dab in the middle of this great battle between good and evil.

So God allowed Satan to do his worst to Job. I mean, in one fell swoop Job lost *everything*: his home, property, riches, children, and health. The only things left were his wife and his friends—and all they did was bad-mouth him, tell him he was sinful, and suggest that he curse God and die. Job wondered what he had done to deserve all of it, but he didn't sin and ultimately passed the test (see Job 2:10).

This is not to say that Job didn't get angry, doubtful, and depressed. I mean, he even cursed the day he was born. He went through a lot of strong emotions and asked God all kinds of questions about pain and suffering. God is big enough to take our big questions, so if you're presently going through something, pour your heart and your emotions out to Him.

God responded and basically let Job know: "I am great, and you are small" (see Job 38-41). God reminded Job that His ways are unknowable and that even though Job didn't understand why it was all happening, God is still bigger than all problems and He's loving, powerful, wise, and faithful. The story ends with God totally restoring everything Job lost—and then some. It also ends with Job telling God these deep words: "No one can oppose you, because you have the power to do what you want. You asked why I talk so much when I know so little. I have talked about things that are far beyond my understanding. You told me to listen and answer your questions. I heard about you from others; now I have seen you with my own eyes" (Job 42:2-5).

God never told Job why these things happened, but reminded Job that He is loving, kind, righteous, and faithful. Job finally understood, as we all must, that while we're on earth God may never reveal why bad things happen to us. The only thing we need to know is that God is faithful and will never leave us alone.

BIG BROTHER IS WATCHING

I just read the most interesting article entitled " 'Big Brother'? No, It's Parents."* The article talks about the increasing ability and frequency with which parents are tracking their children's online movements: whom they meet, what they do, and even what they write.

If people have reached this level of sophistication, why would we be surprised that God has the ability to record not only our actions and our words, but more important, the deepest, darkest, most private thoughts, intentions, and motivations of our hearts.

Jesus said: "I promise you that on the day of judgment, everyone will have to account for every careless word they have spoken. On that day they will be told that they are either innocent or guilty because of the things they have said" (Matthew 12:36, 37). Jesus was talking about the great-white-throne judgment found in Revelation 20:11-15, which will happen for everybody who's ever been alive on this earth.

The prophet Ezekiel, in the Old Testament book named after him, tells an incredible account of a vision he had. In chapter 1 he writes about seeing four living creatures with faces on all four sides of their heads. These creatures were moving in every direction. They had beside them a wheel within a wheel that had rings of eyes all around them, and they could move as quickly as sparks from a fire or lightning. What God allowed Ezekiel to see essentially represented God's system of ever-present communication with His angels, who follow His commands and bring Him information. Big Brother is always watching.

King David asks the question: "Where could I go to escape You, God?" (see Psalm 139:7-18). By the end of this passage he realizes that God is everywhere and knows everything. You can't fool God. Big Brother is always watching. God is all-powerful, all-knowing, and ever-present. We can't hide anything from Him. But this begs the question: Why would we want to? If we're in a right relationship with Him, what have we got to worry about? The only answer I know is simply sin.

Let's look at what sin does right after God's perfect creation. Genesis 3 opens with Satan taking control of a snake. He ultimately lies to everybody and causes Adam and Eve to sin. They realize that they're naked and are ashamed (a negative emotion they've never felt before). This is where we pick up the story:

"Late in the afternoon a breeze began to blow, and the man and woman heard the Lord God walking in the garden. They were frightened and hid behind some trees.

"The Lord called out to the man and asked, 'Where are you?'

"The man answered, 'I was naked, and when I heard you walking through the garden, I was frightened and hid!'

" 'How did you know you were naked?' God asked. 'Did you eat any fruit from that tree in the middle of the garden?'

" 'It was the woman you put here with me,' the man said. 'She gave me some of the fruit, and I ate it.'

"The Lord God then asked the woman, 'What have you done?'

" 'The snake tricked me,' she answered. 'And I ate some of that fruit' " (Genesis 3:8-13).

God knew what caused them to sin, what they did, how they felt, and why they were scared. But like a caring, compassionate parent who's motivated by a loving relationship, He tried to draw out His children's deepest motivations and emotions by asking them to explain. The responses He got from Adam and Eve were initially honest about how they felt. But that's where the honesty stopped. They didn't take responsibility for their behavior and blamed everybody—even God! Sound familiar?

In one fell swoop Adam and Eve went from being God's friends to being His enemies. They went from daily walking and talking with God to being ashamed, feeling afraid of Him, and hiding from Him—and we as humans have been hiding from God ever since.

Sadly, God ended up having to separate Adam and Eve from Himself. Sin always separates. But first He killed an animal in order to give them clothes to wear. This served as a painful and unforgettable reminder of the logical consequences of sin: something had to die because of their sin. And the death of that animal also represented the death of Jesus in our place so we can be clothed in His perfect robe of righteousness and be restored to a right relationship with Him—a relationship in which we no longer have to be ashamed and scared of God, but can "come boldly to the throne of our gracious God" (Hebrews 4:16, NLT).

So are you joyful and bold in God's presence? Are you comfortable with Him watching your every move and knowing your every thought and motivation? Or are you ashamed, scared, and trying to hide from Him? Either way, He knows you and still loves you. Don't make excuses or blame God for your behavior. Repent and confess of your sin right now; remember, Big Brother is always watching. But He's not out to get you. He's out to get your heart.

---

*www.nytimes.com/2012/06/26/technology/software-helps-parents-monitor-their-children-online.html?_r=1&src=me&ref=general&pagewanted=print

THE GRIDIRON OF LIFE

Football players often talk about how games are won and lost in the trenches, the line of scrimmage. Players scratch and claw, push and shove, and run through and over each other just to win the game. The gridiron is the place where the battle is won or lost, the spot where men are tested and proved.

Life today is not much different from football, many say. People are willing to do almost anything to get ahead—or to just make it. Is this truly God's plan for life? Can we find lasting joy, contentment, and peace this way? Was this how we were meant to live? The answer to all of these questions is a resounding no!

God came so that we could have life—and not just a black-and-white-four-inch-TV life, but a full-color-3-D-HD-surround-sound-52-inch-flat-screen-TV life! Jesus put it like this: "A thief [the devil] comes only to rob, kill, and destroy. I [Jesus] came so that everyone would have life, and have it in its fullest" (John 10:10).

Jesus said: "Are you tired? Worn out? Burned out on religion? Come to me. Get away with me and you'll recover your life. I'll show you how to take a real rest. Walk with me and work with me—watch how I do it. Learn the unforced rhythms of grace. I won't lay anything heavy or ill-fitting on you.

Keep company with me and you'll learn to live freely and lightly" (Matthew 11:28-30, Message).

And we can have that full life not just when we get to heaven and everything is perfect—no, we can begin that life right now! The moment you accept Jesus as your Savior and Lord, you can have heaven right here on earth. What does it mean to accept Jesus as both your Savior and Lord? To accept Jesus as your Savior means to accept the fact that there's nothing you can do to save yourself, because you're evil and you've sinned. Don't get your feelings hurt; I'm evil too—we all are! The Bible tells us in Romans 3:23, 24: "All of us have sinned and fallen short of God's glory. But God treats us much better than we deserve [grace], and because of Christ Jesus, he freely accepts us and sets us free from our sins."

And guess what the payment for sin will always be? That's right—you guessed it: death! The Bible plainly states: "Sin pays off with death. But God's gift is eternal life given by Jesus Christ our Lord" (Romans 6:23). The Bible tells us:

"Christ died for us at a time when we were helpless and sinful. No one is really willing to die for an honest person, though someone might be willing to die for a truly good person. But God showed how much he loved us by having Christ die for us, even though we were sinful.

"But there is more! Now that God has accepted us because Christ sacrificed his life's blood, we will also be kept safe from God's anger. Even when we were God's enemies, he made peace with us, because his Son died for us. Yet something even greater than friendship is ours. Now that we are at peace with God, we will be saved by his Son's life. And in addition to everything else, we are happy because God sent our Lord Jesus Christ to make peace with us" (Romans 5:6-11).

Why did Jesus die for us? Here's the answer: "This is how much God loved the world: He gave his Son [Jesus], his one and only Son. And this is why: so that no one need be destroyed; by believing in him, anyone can have a whole and lasting life" (John 3:16, Message).

The second part to that equation—living an abundant life—is achieved through accepting Jesus not just as your Savior, but also as your Lord. In other words, you let Jesus (and God) call the shots with your life and stop fighting Him. I don't know about you, but I'm tired of fighting, kicking, clawing, struggling, and scratching my way over people, relationships, and things. I'm tired of trying to grab as much as I can as fast as I can, thinking that this will help me win in life.

And you know what? In the end we'll find that it's all worthless without an acknowledgment of who God is and obedience to the rules He lays out for our joy, contentment, and peace, both in this life and the next. There was a Jewish king named Solomon—the Bible calls him the wisest person in the world—who spent almost his entire life looking for joy, peace and contentment. Near the end of his life he came to his senses, and this is what he said: "Respect and obey God! This is what life is all about" (Ecclesiastes 12:13).

Are you searching for peace? for joy? for contentment? The apostle Paul wrote something interesting while he was rotting in a stinking jail: "I've learned by now to be quite content whatever my circumstances. I'm just as happy with little as with much, with much as with little. I've found the recipe for being happy whether full or hungry, hands full or hands empty. Whatever I have, wherever I am, I can make it through anything in the One who makes me who I am" (Philippians 4:11-13, Message).

Are you tired of the rat-race gridiron of life? Are you ready to trade it all in for a connection with Christ? Do you want to make it through the game of life with happiness, joy, contentment, and peace with God? You can do it right now by simply accepting the life and death that Jesus gave for you. Why would you wait until the game is over only to find out in the end that you've lost it all—when you can win it all right now?

Do you want to learn more about having a right-now relationship with Jesus? You just need to do two things:

1. Confess (which means "to agree with") to God that you're a sinner and that you'll always be a sinner and that there's nothing you can do by yourself to change.
2. Ask God to apply to you the credit that belongs to Jesus for the perfect life that He lived and the death that He took on your behalf.

In return, God will do two things:

1. He'll forgive your sins: "If we confess our sins to God, he can always be trusted to forgive us and take our sins away" (1 John 1:9).
2. He'll give you an abundant life filled with joy, contentment, and peace: "I give you peace, the kind of peace that only I can give. It isn't like the peace that this world can give. So don't be worried or afraid" (John 14:27).

BE A COOKIE-CUTTER CHRISTIAN

Romans 12:21 says: "Do not be overcome by evil, but overcome evil with good" (NIV). How can we Christians follow God's instruction to do that? People today are more selfish, self-absorbed, isolated, prideful, broken, depressed, and hurting than ever before.

Well, we overcome evil with good by sharing with people the good news that Jesus died for them to give them a future hope of heaven and a heavenly relationship with Him right now. As the popular Christian song says, "People need the Lord!" People need the love and peace that only a deep and intimate relationship with Jesus can give them.

But how do we give the gospel to them? How do we present it in a way that is appealing to them and that doesn't turn them off? To answer that question, I first have to tell you a story about my daughter and raw vegetables.

When my daughter (now 9) was 2, my wife and I read a magazine article that described the health benefits of feeding your children raw foods. My daughter would eat raw fruits enthusiastically, but she wouldn't touch raw vegetables with a 10-foot pole. I decided to be sneaky and hide the raw vegetables in her other food, but she was too smart and found them and threw them down with great disgust. Then I tried something even sneakier. I blended the raw vegetables and mixed them in with her other food. But again her amazing taste buds told on me, and she refused. I was really stumped and ready to give up. My daughter would just have to do without the benefits of raw vegetables.

Then I happened to read the magazine article again and discovered the solution: Don't force them to eat the raw vegetables—get them to *want* to eat them! The author said that young kids love small, brightly colored things that are easy to hold, so she recommended getting cookie cutters in various kid-friendly shapes and cutting the vegetables with them. It worked! My daughter began eating all the raw vegetables we wanted her to—because of the way we presented them to her.

Right now you're saying to yourself, "What does this have to do with sharing the gospel?" Well, I think it's got lots to do with it. Here are Jesus' instructions for sharing the good news of salvation with a dying world:

"Stay alert. This is hazardous work I'm assigning you. You're going to be like sheep running through a wolf pack, so don't call attention to yourselves. Be as cunning as a snake, inoffensive as a dove" (Matthew 10:16, Message). Jesus is saying that He wants us to go and spread the gospel message, and He wants us to be smart about the way we do it—to think carefully about the most effective way to present it.

Now that you've heard my veggie tale, let's get back to my original question: How do we present the good news of the gospel to people in a way that's appealing to them and doesn't turn them off?

We do the same thing I did for my daughter. We present it to them in a form that makes them like it and want more. But in order to do that, we need to get to know them, their lives, their likes and dislikes. We need to become acquainted with their world. We need to take the time to show that we care about them.

That's what Jesus did. He and God the Father and the Holy Spirit created the plan of salvation. Then Jesus came to live among us in poverty before dying on the cross to save us from our sins. The Bible says of Jesus: "In the beginning was the one who is called the Word. The Word was with God and was truly God. From the very beginning the Word was with God. And with this Word, God created all things. Nothing was made without the Word. Everything that was created received its life from him, and his life gave light to everyone. . . . The Word became a human being and lived here with us. We saw his true glory, the glory of the only Son of the Father. From him all the kindness and all the truth of God have come down to us" (John 1:1-14).

Don't you think that after spending 30 years with the human race—as a human being walking among us—Jesus understood us and what makes us tick? Then, and only then, was He ready to begin His ministry, which lasted three and a half years. At the end of that time He died to pay the penalty for every sin ever committed by a human being, so that everyone who has ever chosen to accept His sacrifice could be saved and have eternal life (see John 3:16, 17).

Now, if Jesus was willing to do that for us, and that was His process for bringing salvation to us, how much more should we, His followers, be willing to use His process of identifying with those whom we want to share the gospel message with?

Jesus is coming back soon, and I want to bring as many of my family, friends, and coworkers to Him as I can. It's incredible that Jesus loved us enough to die for us, but it's even more incredible that He trusts us enough to give us the privilege and responsibility of sharing His good news with the rest of the world. He asks you and me to be ambassadors for Him—to tell as many people as we can about His love, peace, forgiveness, joy, and salvation. The apostle Peter says: "The day of the Lord's return will surprise us like a thief. The heavens will disappear with a loud noise, and the heat will melt the whole universe. Then the earth and everything on it will be seen for what they are. Everything will be destroyed. So you should serve and honor God by the way you live. You should look forward to the day when God judges everyone, and you should try to make it come soon" (2 Peter 3:10-12).

So what are you waiting for? Be a cookie-cutter Christian and present the gospel of Jesus to others in all its attractiveness!

DISNEY WORLD DEATH

I grew up in central Florida in the town of Apopka, which is near Orlando. We lived quite close to Walt Disney World. My aunt worked at another amusement park, and several times a year she traded her free employee tickets to her own park for tickets to Disney's Magic Kingdom.

The night before any of our trips to the park, my brothers and I got so excited that it seemed as though we'd never be able to get to sleep. We had the whole trip planned down to a science. We knew the best rides, the best places to eat, and the best times to go anywhere. When we arrived, we ran and ran and ran in the hot Florida sun until the sun went down and we grudgingly had to go home.

Once we got into our van to begin the ride back home, we enthusiastically started talking about all our incredible adventures. But soon we dropped off to sleep in exhaustion. You know the kind of deep sleep I'm talking about.

The next thing we knew, it was morning. Mom and Dad had carried us into the house, put our pajamas on us, and put us into bed—all without our ever waking up. As far as we were concerned, one minute we were in the car leaving the Magic Kingdom at night, and the next minute we were in our beds and it was daytime. How confusing. Has that ever happened to you?

That's what the Bible says death is like: a deep, unconscious, dreamless sleep (see, for example, 1 Kings 2:10; Psalm 13:3; Jeremiah 51:39; Matthew 9:24; and Acts 7:60). It's a state of complete nothingness (see Ecclesiastes 9:5).

A lot of people think that when we die, we either go directly to heaven and spend eternity with God or go directly to hell and spend eternity burning with the devil and his evil angels. But that's not what the Bible teaches. The Bible tells us that when we die, every part of us ceases to exist.

But in the future there will be two different resurrections brought about by God. The first one is only for the righteous dead—those who accepted Christ as their Savior and lived as His loving followers. The second resurrection takes place 1,000 years later. It is only for the wicked dead—those who didn't ultimately accept Christ as their Savior and lived as followers of Satan or the world. Soon after the second resurrection, Satan, his evil angels, and the wicked will be destroyed by fire. They will completely burn up, and then the fire will go out. No one will burn forever. It's just that the results of the fire—their deaths—will be everlasting (see Revelation 20:1-9).

Paul describes the first resurrection in 1 Thessalonians 4:13-18: "Brothers and sisters, we do not want you to be uninformed about those who sleep in death, so that you do not grieve like the rest of mankind, who have no hope. For we believe that Jesus died and rose again, and so we believe that God will bring with Jesus those who have fallen asleep in him. According to the Lord's word, we tell you that we who are still alive, who are left until the coming of the Lord, will certainly not precede those who have fallen asleep [died]. For the Lord himself will come down from heaven, with a loud command, with the voice of the archangel and with the trumpet call of God, and the dead in Christ will rise first. After that, we who are still alive and are left will be caught up together with them in the clouds to meet the Lord in the air. And so we will be with the Lord forever. Therefore encourage one another with these words" (NIV).

Aren't you glad the Bible is clear about what will happen after we die? We won't be in some heavenly waiting room or burning in hell eternally. God is too loving, too kind, and too merciful for that. We'll just be in a state of nothingness—like a deep sleep—waiting for one of the two future resurrections.

However, you may ask, "If God is so loving, then why will He destroy Satan and all the wicked?" Well, the answer is really quite simple. The God who loved Adam and Eve enough to give them the free choice to obey or disobey Him is the same God who created a way to fix the sin problem. If we want to, we can choose eternal life by accepting Jesus as our Savior. Or we can turn down the gift of salvation. The choice that we make with our free will determines whether we spend eternity with God or not.

Here's the bottom line: God loves you so much that He's willing to honor your choice to live your life without Him. But in the end He's still coming back to make all things right and to restore the perfect world that He initially created. If we don't want any part of Him, then as much as He hates to let us go, He'll honor our request. God doesn't want us to be destroyed by fire, but He won't take away our freedom to choose that end.

God says: "Tell them that as surely as I am the living Lord God, I don't like to see wicked people die. I enjoy seeing them turn from their sins and live. So if the Israelites want to live, they must stop sinning and turn back to me" (Ezekiel 33:11).

He's that loving and that fair. God doesn't want worship and obedience that are forced. He wants to spend time with people who want to spend time with Him.

So what choice do you want to make? I'm choosing eternity with God. I hope you'll want to choose the same thing. And you can make that choice right now. Start enjoying life and peace and fellowship with God today!

CLOSED-MINDED CHRISTIAN

Here's a post we received on the *Insight* Web site:

A lot of times I hear people (non-Christians, to be specific) accusing Christians of being judgmental, closed-minded Bible-huggers who refuse to listen to or accept anything of this world that does not pertain to the Bible or Christianity. Sometimes, though, I feel that there are some things in this world that we as Christians should *close our minds to. I feel that it is necessary to an extent to be somewhat closed-minded because there are just too many tricks and traps that Satan has set to drag people down. I'm not implying that we should completely disregard everything that doesn't directly relate to God. I'm saying that I don't think it's downright wrong not to open oneself up to every non-Christian belief or concept that "the world" throws our way. I know for a fact that I would rather be accused of being closed- or narrow-minded and be accepted into God's kingdom than open my mind to every worldly aspect and be deterred from my relationship with God.—Ryan.*

Wow! It sounds as though you must have had a serious discussion, interaction, or disagreement with somebody. Thanks for your straightforward and strong view of God's holiness. I absolutely agree—and disagree—with your position on this topic. Let me explain.

I think it's really important that we make a distinction between non-Christians who have already heard the gospel and have decided not to accept Jesus and non-Christians who either haven't heard the gospel or are still undecided. We also need to consider interacting with those folks who call themselves Christians but who live like non-Christians. With all of these groups it's important to examine how we should respond to them. But before we do that, let's make one thing clear: Our job as Christians on this earth is to spread the good news of salvation to as many people in as many ways as we can.

In Jesus' day there were some people who felt that they shouldn't "dirty" themselves with sinners and that they should hang out with only "perfect," "clean" people. I like to call these folks the "frozen chosen." Let's look at Matthew 9:9-13 and see what Jesus had to say about that: "As Jesus was leaving, he saw a tax collector named Matthew sitting at the place for paying taxes. Jesus said to him, 'Come with me.' Matthew got up and went with him. Later, Jesus and his disciples were having dinner at Matthew's house. Many tax collectors and other sinners were also there. Some Pharisees asked Jesus' disciples, 'Why does your teacher eat with tax collectors and other sinners?' Jesus heard them and answered, 'Healthy people don't need a doctor, but sick people do. Go and learn what the Scriptures mean when they say, "Instead of offering sacrifices to me, I want you to be merciful to others." I didn't come to invite good people to be my followers. I came to invite sinners.'" Yeah! Jesus schooled those folks about the true reason He was there: to offer sick sinners (such as you, me, and everyone else) the true medicine, which is eternal life through Him. And as I mentioned earlier, this is what Jesus' followers are here for too.

Now, Ryan, with that clear, let's talk about how you're both right and wrong. I absolutely agree with you that as Christians we should be extremely careful not to entertain thoughts, ideas, worldviews, or attitudes that are anti-God or anti-truth. James 4:4 tells us: "Don't you know that if you love the world, you are God's enemies? And if you decide to be a friend of the world, you make yourself an enemy of God." Also, Proverbs 4:23 warns: "Carefully guard your thoughts because they are the source of true life."

That being said, though, we should also be careful not to hide ourselves away, being afraid of the ugliness, sin, and evils of this world to the point to which we—the light to the darkness—hide our light. Jesus said: "You are like light for the whole world. A city built on top of a hill cannot be hidden, and no one would light a lamp and put it under a clay pot. A lamp is placed on a lampstand, where it can give light to everyone in the house. Make your light shine, so that others will see the good that you do and will praise your Father in heaven" (Matthew 5:14-16).

If you're talking about angry, stubborn, frothy-mouthed, crazy-eyed, out-to-eat-Christians-for-breakfast non-Christians, then yes, the Bible makes it clear that we should tell them about the gospel. But if they refuse to "hear" (Bible-speak for "change"), well, Jesus told His disciples when He was sending them out to tell others about Him that they should shake the dust off their sandals and leave that place (Matthew 10:13-15). Translation: Leave them alone.

I know, I know, it sounds harsh, but in terms of loving others and living your life, even Jesus understood that people have their own brains and make their own decisions, and if they want to live their lives without God—which is really no life at all—then that's fine. Well, really, it's not fine, but God's not going to force them to accept His salvation; that's not how He rolls.

If you're talking about dealing with non-Christians who've never heard the good news of salvation and who are open and receptive to it, you've got to speak their language. When the apostle Paul was speaking about God calling him into ministry, he clarified this important principle of evangelism: "I am not anyone's slave. But I have become a slave to everyone, so that I can win as many people as possible. When I am with the Jews, I live like a Jew to win Jews. They are ruled by the Law of Moses, and I am not. But I live by the Law to win them. And when I am with people who are not ruled by the Law, I forget about the Law to win them. Of course, I never really forget about the law of God. In fact, I am ruled by the law of Christ. When I am with people whose faith is weak, I live as they do to win them. I do everything I can to win everyone I possibly can. I do all this for the good news, because I want to share in its blessings" (1 Corinthians 9:19-23).

Paul basically said that as Christians we must meet people where they're at. We can't speak "Christianese" to a non-Christian and expect them to get it. Can you imagine how you would feel if you weren't a Christian and someone asked you, "Have you been washed in the blood . . . and been made clean?" What? Excuse me? I'd be calling 9-1-1 immediately and getting out of there as fast as my toothpick legs could take me (cue cartoon Fred Flintstone running sounds).

In terms of dealing with people who call themselves Christians but live like non-Christians, Jesus clearly wants us to steer clear of people like that in our lives. Why? Well, for one, not hanging around with them could serve as a lesson to them that what they're doing isn't OK. And second, the foolishness of these people can pull others in and hook them before they even know it. It's kind of like they have a super-contagious disease that'll mess anyone up who gets near. If you knew you could get really messed up from getting close to them, you'd keep your distance, right?

Now, I'm not talking about a Christian who is trying to live a godly life but keeps making mistakes; no one is perfect. I'm talking about the person who is outright sinning and proud of it. They are unapologetic and may even make fun of you if you don't (and even if you do) go along with the foolishness they've got going on. The apostle Paul, speaking to Christians about this same issue, gave this clear piece of teaching: "In my other letter I told you not to have anything to do with immoral people. But I wasn't talking about the people of this world. You would have to leave this world to get away from everyone who is immoral or greedy or who cheats or worships idols. I was talking about your own people who are immoral or greedy or worship idols or curse others or get drunk or cheat. Don't even eat with them!" (1 Corinthians 5:9-11).

I hope that these guidelines are helpful to you as you try to navigate through the difficult river of living in this world, being involved in others' lives, but not getting sucked into all the crazy and becoming a part of it. In conclusion I leave you with this challenge: "Do not be overcome by evil, but overcome evil with good" (Romans 12:21).

WHY ARE YOU A FIREWORK?

"Cause, baby, you're a firework," my daughter belted from the other room.

I came around the corner just in time to see her rehearsing—in perfect sync with the song—a choreographed dance move that she was learning in her summer drama camp. I stood there, my mouth gaping.

"Come on, let your colors burst . . ."

I was stunned—not that my daughter was singing and dancing, but at what she was singing and dancing to. After picking up my mouth off the floor, I proceeded to sit down and listen to the rest of the lyrics . . . and man, was I blown away! They promoted the same lie that Satan fed Adam and Eve in the garden: you can be like God; better still, you can be your own god. (Needless to say, I did not allow her to perform that song.)

Before we look at the song "Firework," let me share some information about the artist, Katy Perry (aka Katy Hudson). Katy was raised by Christian parents; she listened to only gospel music growing up, and she sang in her local church. As Katy Hudson, she released a gospel album in 2001, which was deemed unsuccessful. Fast-forward several years: After signing with Capitol Music Group in 2007, she adopted the stage name Katy Perry. After she changed her name—and her entire character (it seems) as well—she began releasing all kinds of disgusting and inappropriate music with all kinds of weird and godless messages.

The Christian magazine *Clubhouse* wrote this about her, and I agree: "Soon after that she [Katy Perry] rebelled in a big way and has made a career out of racy songs and shocking behavior. . . . A line on her CD *One of the Boys* asks, 'Have you ever been so lost / known the way and still so lost?' She knows the way. Her parents taught it to her, and she sang about it on her Christian CD."

Now to the song my daughter was singing. "Firework" asks the listener if they've ever felt "like a plastic bag, drifting through the wind." It goes on to describe feelings of hopelessness, worthlessness, and meaninglessness. But then Katy turns and tells the listener that there's something special and original and glowing about each person.

From all appearances Katy is no longer a Christian. That's why she's speaking about "good stuff" that's just naturally inside of us and how we can dream and succeed and overcome—all by ourselves—even when we feel overwhelming sadness, hopelessness, and depression that come from living a sinful human existence. Where do you think we can get the remedy for the sadness and despair that each of us knows? Where is all this "good stuff" coming from?

Well, the devil wants her—and you—to think that it's all inside of us. Don't miss the worldview that's being presented here: We don't need God to be good or to achieve anything extraordinary; all we need to succeed is found inside of us, so all we have to do is look at ourselves and we'll find goodness, even greatness.

The Bible, of course, tells us something different. It tells us that we're all by nature sinful and evil and selfish, that the right and fair response to our sin is death, and that the further we get from God the worse off we'll become (Romans 1; 3:23; and 6:23). Jesus tells us that without God we can do nothing (John 15). The Bible also tells us that God alone can change us in powerful ways (Philippians 4:13), but only through the power of the Holy Spirit, given to us when we accept Jesus—as opposed to any supposed goodness inherent inside us.

So the next time you catch yourself humming, tapping your feet, and singing along to the words of this song, remember that you indeed are a firework. But not because of anything that you've done or anything that you naturally are; you're a firework because of who God is and what He's done for you. In Him, you're a new creation (2 Corinthians 5:17). So be a firework and let your light shine for the whole world to see. And don't let it shine for you, but let it shine for God (see Matthew 5:14; Philippians 2:14, 15).

WHAT TO DO WHEN GOD ASKS YOU TO GIVE UP YOUR DREAM

I want to tell you a story. This is the story of a guy named Abram (later called Abraham). Now, Abram was just an old desert dude minding his own business when God showed up and made him an incredible promise. It's found in Genesis 12:1-9:

"The Lord said to Abram: Leave your country, your family, and your relatives and go to the land that I will show you. I will bless you and make your descendants into a great nation. You will become famous and be a blessing to others. I will bless anyone who blesses you, but I will put a curse on anyone who puts a curse on you. Everyone on earth will be blessed because of you.

"Abram was seventy-five years old when the Lord told him to leave the city of Haran. He obeyed and left with his wife Sarai, his nephew Lot, and all the possessions and slaves they had gotten while in Haran.

"When they came to the land of Canaan, Abram went as far as the sacred tree of Moreh in a place called Shechem. The Canaanites were still living in the land at that time, but the Lord appeared to Abram and promised, 'I will give this land to your family forever.' Abram then built an altar there for the Lord.

"Abram traveled to the hill country east of Bethel and camped between Bethel and Ai, where he built another altar and worshiped the Lord. Later, Abram started out toward the Southern Desert."

What a promise! God told Abram exactly what His dream for him would be, didn't He? That was easy for Abram to know, since he got it straight from God, but what about you and me? What is our God-given dream?

Well, we have to be able to define it before we can know what it is. Simply put, a God-given dream typically flows out of things you enjoy, things that you're good at, or things you have an interest in. A God-given dream can be something that you've always known you would do when you grew up, or a God-given dream can be something you find out about later in life. Either way, God gives us these dreams for three purposes:

1. To ultimately bring honor and glory to God.
2. To make disciples for Him and spread the good news of His grace, mercy, and salvation (aka "the gospel").
3. To bring true and lasting fulfillment, joy, peace, purpose, and power to our lives.

Do you know what your God-given dream is? If you know what it is, the best way to achieve that dream is to get to know God really well, because He created you (and everything else, by the way); therefore, He knows you and what's best for you. If you don't know what your God-given dream is, that's OK too. How do you find out? Just keep on getting to know God better and better; when the time is right, He'll let you know.

OK, now that we've described what a God-given dream is, let's get back to our story. God told Abram that He would bless him and his descendants. That sounds pretty good, doesn't it? Wouldn't you like God to tell you that He'll bless you and that you'll be a blessing to others? But hold on a minute. This promise was not so easy for Abram to believe; you'll see why later on.

God told Abram something to do, and his doing it was vital to the fulfillment of God's promise. Notice what it says in verses 4 and 5: "Abram was seventy-five years old when the Lord told him to leave the city of Haran. He obeyed and left with his wife Sarai, his nephew Lot, and all the possessions and slaves they had gotten while in Haran." What incredible obedience! The Bible doesn't record that Abram questioned or hesitated.

In fact, it records the total opposite: Abram and his family left with all their stuff—just like that.

Do you and I have that kind of faith when all we know is what God told us, but we don't know the plan? Wow! And by the way, here's a little important detail that I don't want you to miss, because it makes Abram's behavior even more incredible: Did you notice that Abram didn't have any children? It's kind of hard to have descendants without, well . . . descendants.

We haven't gotten to the end of our story, but already there are a couple of important things we can learn from Abraham and Sarah's story:

1. God has given you a specific dream to serve Him, increase His kingdom, and bring honor and glory to His name.
2. God will likely not tell you all the details and plans up front; He's looking for you to give Him your total trust and obedience.

I hope that you're really letting this story soak in and that you apply it to your life. Remember what I said before—everything in the Bible is written for a purpose and that is to help you live a better life for God.

In the midst of Abram's journey to find the Promised Land, the Lord reminded Abram several more times of His incredible promise. But don't you know that Abram was human? And don't you know that he was not getting any younger? And don't you know that he must have been thinking a lot about God's promise?

Finally in chapter 15 of Genesis we see Abram verbalizing what must have been on his and his wife's mind the entire time: "Abram answered, 'Lord All-Powerful, you have given me everything I could ask for, except children. And when I die, Eliezer of Damascus will get all I own. You have not given me any children, and this servant of mine will inherit everything' " (verses 2 and 3).

There it is! Isn't it nice to know that Abram was human just like you and me, and questioned and doubted too? God replied to Abram that he indeed would have a child and that his descendants would be like the stars in the heavens. Take a look at Abram's response to God's explanation: "Abram believed the Lord, and the Lord was pleased with Him" (verse 6).

Fast-forward several more years. By this time Abram was trying to make God's promise come true all by himself, in his power, and through his timetable, and it's no surprise that lots of really bad things happened with his family. (I'm talking *The Jerry Springer Show*—everybody in the family needed therapy!)

Here's an interesting question that I can't resist asking you: Have you ever tried to fulfill God's dream for you in your own timetable and through your own power? What were the results? Not good? I know. I've also experienced those same results—for 10 years of my life. And the truth is that every morning I must choose to let God control my moment-by-moment choices so that in the end I will have a good life and can live the dream that God has given me.

In the midst of all this craziness, Abram's wife, Sarai, still hadn't had any children. Abram was again reassured by God of His promise to Abram, and in chapter 18 of Genesis we see God more specifically promise Abram and give a specific time when his son will be born.

Fast-forward many years. In Genesis 22 Abram's name has been changed to Abraham, and his son has been born and probably grown up into a preteen or teen, maybe about your age. Both Abraham and his wife (who, by the way, had her name changed as well from Sarai to Sarah) have passed and failed many faith tests throughout their lives thus far, but God has one final test for Abraham to see if he really loves and trusts God. The story is found in Genesis 22:1-18. We won't look at all the verses, but I encourage you to read it on your own. Here's the bottom line: God decided to test Abraham's trust, loyalty, faith, and obedience to Him and to His promises by asking Abraham to sacrifice—aka kill—his only, promised son! Abraham followed through with total faith in God, and at the last second, literally, he was stopped, Abraham's son was spared, and God provided an animal sacrifice instead.

Let's take a look at several verses to get the flavor of what God was trying to do and Abraham's responses: "The Lord said, 'Go get Isaac, your only son, the one you dearly love! Take him to the land of Moriah, and I will show you a mountain where you must sacrifice him to me on the fires of an altar'" (verse 2). "'Don't hurt the boy or harm him in any way!' the angel said. 'Now I know that you truly obey God, because you were willing to offer him your only son'" (verse 12). "The Lord's angel called out from heaven a second time: 'You were willing to offer the Lord your only son, and so he makes you this solemn promise, "I will bless you and give you such a large family, that someday your descendants will be more numerous than the stars in the sky or the grains of sand along the beach. They will defeat their enemies and take over the cities where their enemies live. You have obeyed me, and so you and your descendants will be a blessing to all nations on earth"'" (verses 15-18).

Wow! Would you be willing to do that? I mean, would you be willing to give God your all? I mean, take what God has placed on your heart for years and years and just sacrifice it—give it up and totally let it go—just because God told you to? Could you do that? Or would you want to hold on to it even harder and stronger? If you do that, it's going to be more painful than ever when God has to rip it out of your hands as opposed to you living your life with your spiritual hands holding loosely to the things of this life and holding tightly only to Jesus.

I've found the secret of holding on to things loosely in this world—even the dreams that God has given me—and it's found in Jeremiah 29:11: " 'For I know the plans I have for you,' declares the Lord" (NIV). So it stands to reason that if I hold on to God and seek to know Him with all my heart, soul, mind, and strength, then I'll know—and more important, receive and achieve—God's dream for me. But it's only through letting God have His way in my life, and that means letting God have it all. The Bible says in Psalm 37:4: "Take delight in the Lord, and he will give you the desires of your heart" (NIV).

Hebrews 11 has some interesting information to share about Abraham's and Sarah's faith in overcoming great odds and in God's final test of Abraham:

"Abraham had faith and obeyed God. He was told to go to the land that God had said would be his, and he left for a country he had never seen. Because Abraham had faith, he lived as a stranger in the promised land. He lived there in a tent, and so did Isaac and Jacob, who were later given the same promise. Abraham did this, because he was waiting for the eternal city that God had planned and built.

"Even when Sarah was too old to have children, she had faith that God would do what he had promised, and she had a son. Her husband Abraham was almost dead, but he became the ancestor of many people. In fact, there are as many of them as there are stars in the sky or grains of sand along the beach. . . .

"Abraham had been promised that Isaac, his only son, would continue his family. But when Abraham was tested, he had faith and was willing to sacrifice Isaac, because he was sure that God could raise people to life. This was just like getting Isaac back from death" (verses 8-19).

Did you catch what that last passage said? When God told Abraham to sacrifice his only son, Abraham was willing to do it and believed that God would and could raise Isaac back from the dead if that's what God had to do to fulfill His promise. Wow, what faith in both God's incredible power and His enduring promises!

Now, there are a few really important points to be learned here:

- God can work to bring about good things even in the midst of your stupid mistakes and bad consequences, because He's God. He has a way of making bad things turn out right.
- God is ultimately concerned about your holiness, and He's willing to do whatever it takes to get and keep your attention, trust, and obedience in order to make and keep you holy.
- God might have to get your attention by testing your obedience and allegiance to Him and to His plans. Because of your stubbornness and knuckleheadedness, He might put you in an uncomfortable situation in which—even for a short time—it seems as if He's asking you to give up your dream. But in actuality, what He's asking you to do is not to give up your dream, but to have total trust in Him and to give up control of making your dream come true. Genesis 22:1-12 makes a great point, and it is this: God wants you to take the thing—that dream that you love dearly more than life itself—and totally trust Him with it.
- God can be trusted with your dreams, your hopes, your aspirations for your life, your relationships, your grades, your sports, your family, and whatever it is you're worried about or that is most important to you or that you have big plans for—God is trustworthy.

I hope you've realized that God has a very special dream that He wants to give to you, and He's ready and willing to make it happen in your lifetime, for your joy, and for His glory. I hope you've paid attention to the mistakes Abraham and Sarah made in trying to force God's hand and make their dreams come true in their own timetable—it never worked for them, and it'll never work for me or you. I hope you realize that God may choose to give you a big test to either find out where your priorities and your heart truly are or correct your path and put you on His path again. Many times chasing our God-given dream can totally eclipse our love for the Dream-giver, and that's not cool with God. And finally, I hope you realize that God ultimately wants and deserves your total allegiance and obedience in whatever you do in your life, because God is trustworthy with everything, especially your dreams.

STOP, DROP, AND ROLL!

I remember where I was the first time I knew what I wanted to be when I grew up. I was in the third grade at Dream Lake Elementary School in Apopka, Florida. Some local firefighters came to talk to us about fire safety. I still remember what they said: If you're ever on fire (and trust me, that was a real possibility for me!), you should stop, drop, and roll.

I was so excited looking at all their gear and then telling my parents when I got home, "I'm gonna be a fireman!" When my parents asked me why, I boldly explained, "Because I want to save people from the fire! I don't want any of them to die!"

I wanted to be a firefighter when I was in the third grade because I wanted to save people from dying, to save them from the fire. I no longer want to be a firefighter, but I still want more than ever to save people from dying the eternal death they will die if they don't accept the salvation that Jesus gave them. And I definitely want to save them from the fires of hell that will burn them up.

As Christians, do you and I have that as our focus? I want to take some time to talk about Jesus' mission. Understanding His mission will refocus us on our purpose as well.

Jesus' mission while He was on this earth was to set people free—spiritually, physically, mentally. Take a look at these passages from the Bible. The first one clearly describes the Messiah's mission when He would come to this earth:

"The Spirit of the Lord God has taken control of me! The Lord has chosen and sent me to tell the oppressed the good news, to heal the brokenhearted, and to announce freedom for prisoners and captives. This is the year when the Lord God will show kindness to us and punish our enemies. The Lord has sent me to comfort those who mourn, especially in Jerusalem" (Isaiah 61:1-3).

In this next passage we see Jesus in the synagogue formally announcing His mission and ministry for all—including the Pharisees and Sadducees. Jesus opened the scroll and read from the passage that we just read in Isaiah:

"The Lord's Spirit has come to me, because he has chosen me to tell the good news to the poor. The Lord has sent me to announce freedom for prisoners, to give sight to the blind, to free everyone who suffers, and to say, 'This is the year the Lord has chosen'" (Luke 4:18, 19).

Let's take a look at what Jesus was saying. This is the first time He publicly and formally announced His ministry here on earth. His mission was fivefold:

1. Preach good news to the poor.
2. Proclaim freedom for the prisoners.
3. Give sight to the blind.
4. Release the oppressed.
5. Proclaim the year of the Lord's favor.

Remember, Jesus was making clear that He as the Messiah was not there to build a flashy, violent kingdom that would free the Jews from Roman rule. Jesus didn't come to focus on helping and hanging out with the elite. Instead, Jesus came to look out for all people, specifically focusing on those segments of society that were forgotten, weak, or sick, or couldn't stand up for themselves (some examples of this would be homeless people, widows, orphans, prisoners, etc.). This made some people really mad—so much so that they wanted to kill Him!

In this next passage of Scripture Jesus is making absolutely clear why He hates it when people try to make it on their own steam and change the mission of the church to what they think the church should or shouldn't do.

Here's some background: The Pharisees and the Sadducees were the spiritual leaders in Jesus' day. Jesus had had multiple dealings with them. They had consistently tried to trick Him into saying something to perjure Himself. Incidentally, these religious leaders had already planned multiple times to kill Jesus. Let's see what Jesus said to them regarding what they considered important versus what He thinks is important:

"You Pharisees and teachers are show-offs, and you're in for trouble! You give God a tenth of the spices from your garden, such as mint, dill, and cumin. Yet you neglect the more important matters of the Law, such as justice, mercy, and faithfulness. These are the important things you should have done, though you should not have left the others undone either. You blind leaders! You strain out a small fly but swallow a camel. You Pharisees and teachers are show-offs, and you're in for trouble! You wash the outside of your cups and dishes, while inside there is nothing but greed and selfishness. You blind Pharisee! First clean the inside of a cup, and then the outside will also be clean" (Matthew 23:23-26).

Don't miss it. Jesus was upset because these were the leaders everybody looked up to as examples. But what were they doing? They were being total hypocrites. They would give a tenth (a tithe) of all their personal spices, but they would do nothing to help those who were poor or hurting, or those who had been treated unfairly. Jesus was getting on the religious leaders because they would typically take linen gauze, or probably something similar to cheesecloth, and strain gnats or flies out of their food and drink (because those bugs were unclean), but they themselves were unclean inside! Such hypocrisy! The bottom line is this: If we as Christians know better, we should do better.

Social injustice should make us angry, and we should do something about it. As Christians we should let our love inform how we interact with those people in our sphere of influence who are poor, helpless, sick, or imprisoned—and not in a position to help us or do something for us in return for our kind acts. We can't expect non-Christians to do something for them, because they're typically too wrapped up in themselves. That's who sinners are: they're selfish. But Christians aren't selfish—at least we're not supposed to be!

So let me ask you something: What kind of Christian are you? Are you the kind who talks more than acts? Are you like the Pharisees and Sadducees, who got upset with Jesus and tried to kill Him because He was serving people—I mean, really serving them, asking nothing from them in return and making the leaders look bad as a result? Do you get upset or jealous when you see the good deeds that others are doing for others? Or do you feel guilty? If you do, what do you do with that guilt? Do you reassess things and then do something positive, something to help somebody?

You may not have access to somebody who is physically sick, or a widow, or an orphan, or in jail, but ask yourself this: Whom has God placed within your circle of influence? Are there friends you could help? Is there some kind of homeless shelter you could volunteer at? Is there someone younger than you whom you could mentor? Is there someone older than you whom you could visit or help—or just call to check in on? How about those students who aren't that popular, or those who are socially awkward and bullied? Is there something you can do?

Jesus said of Christians: "You are the light of the world." But did you know that He also called us salt? In Matthew 5:13 Jesus said: "You are like salt for everyone on earth. But if salt no longer tastes like salt, how can it make food salty? All it is good for is to be thrown out and walked on."

What kind of salt are you? Do you taste like salt or just look like it? Are you the real thing? If you are, don't wait to be thrown out because you're no longer useful; it's time for Christians to get out of the saltshaker and into the food!

WHAT TO DO WHEN YOU'RE NOT SURE HOW TO SHARE YOUR FAITH

I'd like to talk about the second-most-important thing we're supposed to do while we're on this earth: evangelism. By the way, the first thing is to accept, know, and love Jesus more and more every day. If we do that, then naturally we'll want to share His love with others . . . right?

Not necessarily so. I want to tell you an interesting and funny Bible story about one of my heroes—Moses. There are a lot of great things we can learn from this story concerning our own relationship with God and the lame excuses we give Him when we don't accept our responsibility to share His good news. I understand that many of us may not do it because we feel ill-equipped, may fear rejection, or are not sure how to do it. But how are we to respond when we don't *want* to share God's good news of salvation? What does that say about us? What does that say about our heart and ultimately our relationship to our God?

Before we jump into the story, let's review who Moses was and get some background info on what was going on. Moses' life was divided neatly into three separate 40-year periods. During the first 40 years Moses was in Egypt learning to be Moses and realizing that he was a Jew; during the second 40 years Moses was in the desert unlearning how to be Moses and learning how to obey God; during the third 40-year period Moses was busy leading God's people out of slavery, wandering in the desert, and teaching them how to obey God.

Moses was the adopted son of Pharaoh, the king of Egypt and the ruler of a large part of the world. Moses was a Jew by birth, and God placed him in Egypt to get the best upbringing and education that anybody could have. To make a long story short, Moses realized that he was a Jew (and Jews were slaves in Egypt), murdered another Egyptian, got busted, became a criminal, and took off from Egypt into the desert, fearing for his life. Moses eventually got married, had some kids, and settled down to tend his father-in-law's herd of sheep. Little did he know how much his sheepherding skills would come in handy when leading all those people through the desert for 40 years! This is where we pick up the story:

"One day, Moses was taking care of the sheep and goats of his father-in-law Jethro, the priest of Midian, and Moses decided to lead them across the desert to Sinai, the holy mountain. There an angel of the Lord appeared to him from a burning bush. Moses saw that the bush was on fire, but it was not burning up. 'This is strange!' he said to himself. 'I'll go over and see why the bush isn't burning up.'

"When the Lord saw Moses coming near the bush, he called him by name, and Moses answered, 'Here I am.'

"God replied, 'Don't come any closer. Take off your sandals—the ground where you are standing is holy. I am the God who was worshiped by your ancestors Abraham, Isaac, and Jacob.'

"Moses was afraid to look at God, and so he hid his face.

"The Lord said:

"I have seen how my people are suffering as slaves in Egypt, and I have heard them beg for my help because of the way they are being mistreated. I feel sorry for them, and I have come down to rescue them from the Egyptians.

"I will bring my people out of Egypt into a country where there is good land, rich with milk and honey. I will give them the land where the Canaanites, Hittites, Amorites, Perizzites, Hivites, and Jebusites now live. My people have begged for my help, and I have seen how cruel the Egyptians are to them. Now go to the king! I am sending you to lead my people out of his country.

"But Moses said, 'Who am I to go to the king and lead your people out of Egypt?'

"God replied, 'I will be with you. And you will know that I am the one who sent you, when you worship me on this mountain after you have led my people out of Egypt.' Moses answered, 'I will tell the people of Israel that the God their ancestors worshiped has sent me to them. But what should I say, if they ask me your name?'

"God said to Moses:

"I am the eternal God. So tell them that the Lord, whose name is 'I Am,' has sent you. This is my name forever, and it is the name that people must use from now on" (Exodus 3:1-15).

Three points will serve as the foundation for what we will discuss:

1. God wants us to share the gospel with as many people as we can

in as many ways as we can! Jesus, right before He took the "holy express elevator" to heaven, clearly gave His disciples—and by extension us—an assignment. "Jesus came to them and said: 'I have been given all authority in heaven and on earth! Go to the people of all nations and make them my disciples. Baptize them in the name of the Father, the Son, and the Holy Spirit, and teach them to do everything I have told you. I will be with you always, even until the end of the world' " (Matthew 28:18-20).

2. God will never leave us or forsake us. (See Matthew 28:20 above.)

3. There is no "plan B" for the spreading of the gospel, aka good news. We're it! Each one of us has the responsibility to share God's love and salvation with as many people as we can. Second Corinthians 5:18-20 puts it like this: "All this is from God, who reconciled us to himself through Christ and gave us the ministry of reconciliation: that God was reconciling the world to himself in Christ, not counting people's sins against them. And he has committed to us the message of reconciliation. We are therefore Christ's ambassadors, as though God were making his appeal through us" (NIV).

As I read through this passage of Scripture, I realized two really important things:

1. God Himself heard the cries of the people, who were in bondage to slavery. Now, you don't have to have your fancy-schmancy doctoral degree from a seminary or university to make the connection between the literal land of Egypt and the figurative land of sin. I find it interesting that God told Moses in Exodus 3:7-9 that He not only had heard the people in slavery crying but was concerned about their suffering. I have just one question based upon that observation: Are you and I concerned about the suffering of the people around us? Do we hear the crying of our family and friends who may be stuck in their own spiritual Egypt and their plea for help from the slavery of sin? Are we concerned? Do we care? If so, what are we doing about it? If we don't, does it bother us that it doesn't bother us?
2. There's an important distinction that God makes here, and it's found in Exodus 3:10: "So now, go. I am sending you to Pharaoh to bring my people the Israelites out of Egypt" (NIV). Did you catch that? In verses 7-9 of Exodus 3 God clearly states that He will set His people free, but then in verse 10 He flips the script and tells Moses, "I will set the slaves free *through you!*"

At this point, Moses begins to give God some pretty lame excuses (see Exodus 4:1-17). Although this story happened a really long time ago, I think you'll see some striking and scary similarities between the reasons—or excuses—that Moses gave and ones that we give. Let's take a look at each one in detail:

1. Moses shares his first excuse, and it's a shocker! Exodus 3:11 shows his response to God: "Who am I that I should go to Pharaoh and bring the Israelites out of Egypt?" Now, remember what happened in the first 40 years of Moses' life? He was in line to be ruler of one of the most powerful nations in the world at that time. And now he was saying "Who am I?"

   I'm glad that God was effective in His job, because I'm sure that while Moses was being raised in Egypt he was full of himself and probably real arrogant. It took him being in the desert and herding sheep for 40 years to break him of his self-focus. Yet Moses went too far; in effect, what Moses was saying was "I'm nobody!" By the way, that's very true, but look at God's response in the following verse: "I will be with you" (verse 12).

   In effect, God reminded Moses: "I know you're nobody, and I'm glad you finally learned that, but don't forget: I'm somebody!" Aren't you glad that God has got your back? To further drive the point home, in verse 14 of Exodus 3 God tells Moses to encourage the other leaders and remind them of God's true name: "I AM WHO I AM." In other words, there is no further intro needed when you talk about God. God is . . . God! He is sufficient for whatever you need Him to be. God is your friend, your judge, your protector, your father, your provider.
2. In Exodus 4:1 we find Moses' second lame excuse, and it's this: "What if they do not believe me or listen to me?" God essentially answers, "I'll make them believe" (see Exodus 4:2-9), which is basically an extension of His first response: "I AM." Remember, it's our responsibility to speak and share—and God's responsibility to do the rest.

   The apostle Paul said it like this: "I [Paul] planted the seeds [the gospel], Apollos watered them [shared more about the gospel], but God made them sprout and grow [God convicted people of the truth of the gospel and brought them to make a decision to accept

Jesus]. What matters isn't those who planted or watered, but God who made the plants grow" (1 Corinthians 3:6, 7).

3. In Exodus 4:10 we find Moses' third and final lame excuse: "I have never been a good speaker. I wasn't one before you spoke to me, and I'm not one now. I am slow at speaking, and I can never think of what to say." In other words, Moses said: "I can't speak well, and I don't know what to say."

How many of us use that same excuse? I know I have in the past. I say such things as "I've never been to seminary" or "I don't know what to say or how to say it." But look at God's response: "The Lord answered, 'Who makes people able to speak or makes them deaf or unable to speak? Who gives them sight or makes them blind? Don't you know that I am the one who does these things? Now go! When you speak, I will be with you and give you the words to say" (verses 11 and 12). In other words, God again says the same thing: "I will be with you and tell you what to say."

Even after God gave Moses reassurance after reassurance of His persistent and powerful presence, Moses point-blank chickened out and point-blank refused. Look at this: "Moses begged, 'Lord, please send someone else to do it' " (verse 13). What? After all that, this is Moses' response? God's response is just like that of any parent who has patiently tried to give their kids all their support: "The Lord became irritated with Moses and said: What about your brother Aaron, the Levite? I know he is a good speaker" (verse 14).

Here's the bottom line: God is going to make sure that the task of evangelism is completed with or without us. Then in verse 15 God again reminds Moses and his brother, Aaron, that He will be with both of them as they speak and He will tell each of them what to do. I find it very interesting that God will not make both of them speak, but will tell them what to say and do. You see, God does not demand our service; He could force us to serve Him, but then we would be nothing more than robots; or He could threaten to kill or injure us, but then we would be serving Him out of fear. No, He wants us to serve Him out of sheer love, thankfulness, and gratitude for who He is and for the great sacrifice He gave for us (Jesus dying on the cross).

Of course, you know how the story ends. Moses and Aaron finally go to speak with Pharaoh, but not before more excuses. It ends with the Israelites being freed from slavery—and then it turns bad again with the

Israelites failing to trust God and wandering in the desert for 40 years as payment for their lack of trust, obedience, and faith.

So what can we learn from this story that we can apply to our own lives? First, God is ultimately in control, and His plans will come to pass with or without us. If we aren't involved in God's plans, I promise you that 100 percent of the time we'll be on the losing end of things. Second, we are nobodies, but God is somebody, and He will always go with us and never leave us, and will tell us what to say and do. As my grandmother used to say: "God is not in the habit of embarrassing Himself."

So if you have an opportunity to evangelize, don't be like Moses and whine and complain; say a quick prayer and move forward in faith and trust, and God will be with you and tell you what to do. Remember, with God you can't go wrong.

WORLDVIEW WARS

What does the term *worldview* mean? A worldview is, well, how you view the world. This affects not only how you live your life, but how you share your faith.

The apostle Paul warns us in Colossians 2:8: "Don't let anyone capture you with empty philosophies and high-sounding nonsense that come from human thinking and from the spiritual powers of this world, rather than from Christ" (NLT). We need to be very careful that we don't think ourselves out of our faith and right into hell.

I'm not telling you that you shouldn't study different faiths and what others believe; after all, how else are we to win people over if we don't know where they're coming from (Acts 17:16-34)? All I'm saying is that you need to be careful to be well grounded in your Christian faith, constantly praying for wisdom when reading and studying, and bouncing information off of people grounded in their Christian faith. I speak from experience: I spent the better part of 10 years being fooled by "empty philosophies and high-sounding nonsense."

Now, the Chuck Colson Center for Christian Worldview provides a helpful explanation of what worldviews are all about:

"Every human being has a worldview, a framework for understanding and interacting with the physical world, other humans, and the Divine.

"Every worldview tells a story—an explanation of life and our place in it—that makes sense to the one who holds it.

"The story line of a worldview typically answers five questions: Where did we come from? What kind of beings are we? Why are we in our condition? How do we improve our condition? Where is all this headed?

"In the Christian worldview these answers come to us by revelation from God, as He speaks to us from His Word, the Bible:

- **WHENCE?** God made us and all things.
- **WHAT?** We are His creatures, and human beings are His image-bearers.
- **WHY?** The creation suffers, and so do people, because of the fall into sin.
- **HOW?** The only way out of our sinfulness into a renewed, restored, and abundant life is through the redemption accomplished by Jesus Christ.
- **WHERE?** Ultimately Jesus will bring His followers home to dwell with Him in a new heaven and new earth, where righteousness dwells."*

Do you remember my discussion of the Katy Perry song "Firework" and the worldview behind it? We saw that the worldview behind the singer was one that was focused not on God but on herself—on human beings, to be more exact. That worldview is called humanism, and it comes in many forms. Many Eastern religions appeal to the same lie, which basically states that everything you need is in you, and if you work hard enough, there's nothing you can't achieve. In other words, you don't need anyone; you can handle things all by yourself, and you have what it takes to get things done.

We need to be careful about what worldview we hold or admire, because our thinking controls our beliefs, and both these elements control our behavior. Here's the bottom line: If we want to behave like Christians, we've got to start thinking and believing like Christians.

Paul wrote: "I am not anyone's slave. But I have become a slave to everyone, so that I can win as many people as possible. When I am with the Jews, I live like a Jew to win Jews. They are ruled by the Law of Moses, and I am not. But I live by the Law to win them. And when I am with people who are not ruled by the Law, I forget about the Law to win them. Of course, I never really forget about the law of God. In fact, I am ruled by the law of Christ. When I am with people whose faith is weak, I live as they do to win them. I do everything I can to win everyone I possibly can. I do all this for the good news, because I want to share in its blessings" (1 Corinthians 9:19-23).

Don't misinterpret this. Paul was not saying that it's OK to totally throw out your own beliefs and act like everybody else whenever you feel like it because your Christian beliefs aren't important. No, he was saying the opposite: Our beliefs are so important that we attempt to understand where other people are coming from (their worldviews) so that we meet them where they are, begin to build relational bridges, and then share Jesus with them! We can't expect people to come to us just because we're Christians, can we? We have to try to understand what makes them tick. This is the whole "fishers of men" thing Jesus was talking about.

The world's worldviews are in collision with ours. Thus, we should know at least something about the worldviews that are central to the conflict.

Look, let me be honest with you: this will be like reading a textbook . . . and I won't apologize for it, because I want you to understand that if you want to reach other people with the gospel, you've got to do some "homework" to understand who they are and what they believe. There, I've said it, and I feel better.

Come on, it won't be that bad. I know you'll learn a lot, and God will be able to use you to bless others through the information you've learned.

The most influential worldviews are (in no particular order): Christian theism, deism, naturalism, nihilism, existentialism, and New Age pantheism or New Consciousness.

DEISM, an important worldview during the eighteenth century, has almost entirely left the scene. The deist believes that God exists, but He created and then abandoned the universe. A famous deist we all know well was Benjamin Franklin. And William Miller, a founder of the Advent movement in the 1830s, was once a deist.

NIHILISM, a more recent worldview, is alive among many young people and some intellectuals (aka eggheads). Nihilists see no value in reality. To them, life is absurd.

EXISTENTIALISM is prominent and can be seen frequently, even among some Christians who don't *think* they are existentialists. The existentialist, like the nihilist, sees life as absurd, but sees humans as totally free to create themselves in the face of this absurdity. Here we see Satan's Garden of Eden lie rearing its ugly head: "You shall be like God."

Christian theism, naturalism, and New Age pantheism are currently the most influential worldviews in the United States. We'll look more closely at each of them:

Christian theists believe that an infinite, personal God created the universe out of nothing. Humans were originally created good in God's image, but chose to sin, thereby infecting all of humanity with what is called a "sin nature." So humans are endowed with value by their Creator, but their sinful nature causes rebellious behavior. Death is the gate to either eternal life with God or eternal separation from Him. The destination is dependent upon the response we give to God's provision for our sinfulness.

The guidelines for our conduct are revealed by God, and God is the only being who can tell us what is ultimately right or wrong. Our reason and our experience through the five senses can be legitimate teachers, but an immutable, transcendent source (someone or something outside of ourselves that never changes) is necessary. We know the most important things only because we are told them by God, mainly through the Bible and His Holy Spirit. History is linear (goes in a straight line) and is a meaningful sequence of events leading the human race to the fulfillment of God's purposes.

Christian theism has a long history in Western culture. However, this does not mean that all people who have ever lived in Western culture have been Christians. It simply means that this worldview was once the most influential and dominant, even among non-Christians. But this is no longer the case. Western culture has experienced a transition to a worldview called naturalism.

Even though naturalism in various forms is ancient, we will use the term to refer to a worldview that has recently risen to considerable influence in a relatively short time within Western culture. The seeds were planted in the seventeenth century and began to flower in the eighteenth. Most of us have been exposed to naturalism through what is called secular humanism.

THE BASIC PRINCIPLES OF THIS WORLDVIEW ARE:

1. God is irrelevant. This idea is the direct opposite of Christian theism, which is based on supernaturalism (whatever is outside of the natural).
2. Progress and evolutionary change are inevitable.
3. Humans are autonomous and self-centered and will save themselves.
4. Education is the guide to life; intelligence and freedom guarantee full human potential.
5. Science is the ultimate provider for both knowledge and morals.

These principles have permeated our lives. They are apparent, for example, in the media, government, and education today. Remember what Paul said to the Colossians? "Don't let anyone capture you with empty philosophies and high-sounding nonsense that come from human thinking and from the spiritual powers of this world, rather than from Christ" (Colossians 2:8). We should be constantly alert and on guard for the influence of naturalistic principles.

After World War II, postmodernism began to replace naturalism. Postmodernism is the idea that truth, in any real and absolute sense, doesn't exist. This appears to be the next major worldview that is taking hold of our culture. It is very popular in high schools and on college campuses.

At the same time, though, the past few decades have brought to us another ancient worldview, dressed up in Western clothing: New Age pantheism.

Various forms of pantheism have been prominent in Eastern cultures for thousands of years. But it began to have an effect on our culture in the 1950s. It took the form of what became known as the New Age movement. When I learned and taught martial arts, I was introduced to and involved in a lot of this type of thinking and philosophy, and for many years I struggled to combine these beliefs with Christian theism . . . and couldn't. I ended up getting entangled in the New Age ideas of pantheism.

WHAT ARE THE BASIC PRINCIPLES OF THE PANTHEIST WORLDVIEW?

1. All is one. There are no ultimate distinctions between humans, animals, or the rest of creation.
2. Since all is one, all is god. All of life has a spark of divinity.
3. If all is one and all is god, then each of us is god.
4. Humans must discover their own divinity by experiencing a change in consciousness. That's why a lot of people do things such as yoga and transcendental meditation.
5. Humans must travel through unending cycles of birth, death, and reincarnation in order to work off what is called "bad karma."

New Age disciples think in terms of gray, not black and white. Thus they believe, like the postmodernist, that two conflicting statements can both be true.

On the popular level, these tenets of belief are presently asserted through media such as books, magazines, television shows, and movies. Perhaps the most visible teacher is George Lucas, creator of the *Star Wars* movies that became so popular. But these beliefs are also found increasingly among intellectuals in fields such as medicine, psychology, sociology, and education.

Now that you've learned about the major worldviews, what will you do with the information? I'm hoping that as you interact with others, read stuff, or watch TV, you'll be more alert to how sneaky the devil is. But even more, I hope you'll learn how you can bridge the differences between you and another person in order to share the lifesaving truth and awesome hope of the gospel of Jesus Christ!

---

*www.colsoncenter.org/search-library/framework-of-truth

UNAPOLOGETIC ABOUT APOLOGETICS

I remember the first time I talked about what I believed to somebody who didn't agree with me. We argued about the Sabbath, and man, I was so right and he was so wrong! But in my rightness I was outright rude and obnoxious.

How did it end? Well, let's just say that I won the argument but lost an opportunity to make a friend, and, more important, lost an opportunity to have a continuing discussion with that person over what makes us the same or different. You see, I totally missed the chance not only to evangelize but also to use apologetics.

You may ask, "What is apologetics?" I'll define it shortly, but first I want to discuss what evangelism is, and then I hope you'll be able to see the similarities and differences between them.

In the previous chapter we talked about the importance of worldviews. In short, a worldview is the way that somebody views the world—and we can't truly evangelize the world until we understand how others view it.

Think about it this way: Jesus said that He came to make us fishers of men, and as fishers we must study and understand whatever we're trying to "catch." So understanding someone's worldview is like understanding the types of things that attract a certain fish. Evangelism is the appropriate baiting of the hook. Apologetics is the struggle with the fish to reel them in.

I used to think that my job as a Seventh-day Adventist Christian was to make other Seventh-day Adventist Christians, but that's not what Jesus said when He gave His disciples their last assignment. Jesus told them (and us) to make disciples. You see, it's our job as Christians not only to share the truth with the world but also to make the truth as clear as possible and work to remove any barriers and/or misunderstandings that people may have. We can't just be like "See, world, we have the truth, and either you can accept it lock, stock, and barrel or you can burn in hell—and by the way, Jesus loves you!" No! We are not to be the way I was in my argument about the Sabbath.

Of course, as Christians we're not to apologize to the world for being who we are. In fact, apologetics is completely the opposite of that. "Apologetic" is a fancy name for the legitimate arguments we make about the gospel. We not only inform others of the good news of the gospel (evangelism) but also defend it in a way that is true, correct, kind, and intelligent (apologetics). As Christians, we are clearly expected to be prepared to give this defense of our faith in any situation.

The most obvious command for an apologetic (aka defense of our faith) is 1 Peter 3:15, 16: "Always be prepared to give an answer to everyone who asks you to give the reason for the hope that you have. But do this with gentleness and respect, keeping a clear conscience, so that those who speak maliciously against your good behavior in Christ may be ashamed of their slander" (NIV).

There are different types of apologetics, but the one that makes the most sense to me is "presuppositional." Presuppositional apologetics assumes that life begins to make sense only when it is considered with a Christian perspective—or worldview—in mind. Once you "presuppose" that Christianity is true, everything else begins to make sense.

Wait one minute, though. This presupposition does not imply that an apologetic defense cannot change the mind of someone who presupposes that there is no God or Christ (atheist) or the mind of someone who presupposes that God just created the earth and planets, wound them up like a clock and let 'em go, and doesn't care about what happens to us (deist). In every case when we begin the process of arguing (kindly, respectfully, and gently), it is God and only God who ultimately brings around the heart of the hardened person to Him, working through us. (Thus the command for us to have a ready defense for what we believe.) In the study of apologetics we confirm our faith both for ourselves and for others who are truly searching for the truth.

Now, apologetics should seek to answer what I like to call the "Big Five Questions." In my experience, these have historically been the questions that most people have the most difficult time with and that keep them from becoming Christians—or coming anywhere near Christianity. They just can't get over these. They are as follows:

1. **TRUTH:** Does absolute, universal truth exist?
2. **GOD:** Can we know that He exists?
3. **SCRIPTURE:** How can we be sure that the Bible is trustworthy?
4. **JESUS:** Is He really the one and only Savior?
5. **PAIN:** Why does a supposedly loving God allow pain and suffering in the world?

People need the love and peace that only a deep and intimate relationship with Jesus can give them. But how do we present it in a way that is appealing to them and doesn't immediately turn them off? We present it to them in a form that they can understand. But in order to do that, we have to get to know them—their lives, their likes and dislikes, their culture. This doesn't mean that we have to be like them, act like them, talk like them, or dress like them. But it does mean that we have to enter their world and attempt to see it through their eyes.

Jesus did the same thing. After He, God the Father, and God the Holy Spirit got together and came up with the plan of salvation, Jesus came to this earth and was born poor, by an unmarried teenage mother on the wrong side of the tracks. The Bible says in John 1:1-4: "In the beginning was the one who is called the Word. The Word was with God and was truly God. From the very beginning the Word was with God. And with this Word, God created all things. Nothing was made without the Word. Everything that was created received its life from him, and his life gave light to everyone." And then verse 14 says: "The Word became a human being and lived here with us. We saw his true glory, the glory of the only Son of the Father. From him all the kindness and all the truth of God have come down to us."

When we read in Acts 17 the story of the apostle Paul talking to non-Christians in Athens, we can learn a lot of things. Before we get into the story, let me give you some background. The apostle Paul—previously known as Saul the Pharisee—and his friends Luke, Silas, and Timothy have set out on Paul's second missionary journey. It seems that Paul caused riots and uproar wherever he went. The reason people got upset with him was that he refused to water down the gospel. He was worried about pleasing only one person: Jesus Christ!

Most recently Paul had caused a riot in the city of Thessalonica, and he and his team had to be sent to Berea for their own safety. But again his preaching and his presence caused quite a stir, and he had to again be moved for his own safety, this time to Athens. However, things got so hairy this time that Paul had to go away by himself.

Here's where we pick up the story—in Acts 17:16-34. I want you to read it for yourself first.

Have you read it? Great! Now let's unpack this really interesting story. The first thing we learn is that we need to care enough about people to be concerned that they will die without a love relationship with Jesus Christ (verse 16).

Paul was really bothered by what he was seeing in Athens. Everywhere he looked he saw idols, and that wasn't cool! The NIV translates it like this: "While Paul was waiting for them in Athens, he was greatly distressed to see that the city was full of idols." How about you? Do you get really upset or bothered by all the sin, death, disease, and dysfunction you see in the world? How about in your school, church, or community? How about with your friends or your family? It's easy just to plug in the MP3 player and say to yourself, "Hey, it's all good. It's none of my business." Aren't you glad that God didn't say that about the sin problem in this world? Or that He doesn't say that about you or me or your parents or friends?

The second thing we can learn from this story is that we should be ready with an effective defense of our faith anywhere and anytime. Don't miss it: Paul was hanging out and waiting for his evangelistic team to arrive when he was thrust before a group of people and asked to speak about his faith. Paul didn't take Jesus' command to spread the gospel and limit it to one day a week—and neither should we. Paul was always sharing Jesus, whether he was standing in front of a group of people or speaking to one person. It didn't matter to him whether he was free or in jail; he was always focused on evangelism. This wasn't just his job—it was who he was! What a powerful lesson we can learn from Paul: evangelism and apologetics are not activities we do one day of the week; they are a lifestyle that we must decide to live day in and day out.

The Bible tells us in 1 Peter 3:15: "Always be prepared to give an answer to everyone who asks you to give the reason for the hope that you have" (NIV). How are people going to hear the gospel if you and I don't present it? It's real important that you understand that God may open a way for you to say something at the drop of a hat, and that's why you've got to know and recognize God's voice (which means that you've got to spend time listening to Him).

The third thing we can learn from this story is that when you share the gospel, understand that there will always be people who disagree with you—and sometimes they'll be very angry and even verbally abusive! "Some of them [philosophers] were Epicureans and some were Stoics, and they started arguing with him. People were asking, 'What is this know-it-all trying to say?' Some even said, 'Paul must be preaching about foreign gods! That's what he means when he talks about Jesus and about people rising from death.' They brought Paul before a council called the Areopagus" (Acts 17:18, 19).

Have you ever heard the saying "Don't shoot the messenger"? Remember this when you attempt to defend your faith. People sometimes get crazy mad at you and will even threaten you with physical violence. I find it interesting that in today's culture of tolerance, people want the freedom to express themselves in any way, shape, or form, but you just can't talk about Jesus!

If you call yourself a Christian and seek to spread the gospel in your everyday life, get ready, because the ugly is coming at you! You might be surprised to know that the world doesn't hate you, but what they hate is the Jesus in you! Don't believe me? Jesus told His followers right before He was about to leave them to be crucified that they shouldn't be surprised that the world will treat them like garbage because that's how the world treated Him too (John 15:18-22). It's no fun, but the ugly truth is that you will receive resistance when you share the truth. But be faithful to what God has called you to do. Don't give up hope.

The fourth thing you can learn from this story will bring you hope, and it's this: the Holy Spirit will open up incredible opportunities for you to share your faith in an even greater and larger way, whether it be through those people you've spoken to who then share with people they know, or, as in Paul's case, through more opportunities to share with the same people and explain things further. Look at verses 19-21 in Acts 17: "And [they] said, 'Tell us what your new teaching is all about. We have heard you say some strange things, and we want to know what you mean.' More than anything else the people of Athens and the foreigners living there loved to hear and to talk about anything new."

Now, Athens, with its magnificent buildings and many gods, was a center for Greek culture, philosophy, and education. Philosophers and educated men were always ready to hear something new, so they invited Paul to speak to them at the meeting of the Areopagus, a kind of council or court. The Areopagus was the place where all the smart people in the city came together. They met on a low hill in Athens near the Acropolis. This was the local Starbucks, if you will. The greatest minds of that day and the most influential thought leaders in that society invited Paul to come and talk to them.

Jesus said: "On my account you will be brought before governors and kings as witnesses to them and to the Gentiles" (Matthew 10:18, NIV). You never know what will happen when you are obedient to what God tells you to do. But one thing I know for sure: We don't ever know how the message we share with somebody will affect them, but we've got to share with them, because if we don't, then who will?

You've got to have done your homework and prayerfully and diligently sought to understand where people are coming from, what their issues are, what their culture is—basically, you've got to understand what makes them tick. Here's the bottom line: When we share and defend the gospel, we should always do it within a context that is familiar to our listener(s). As you read the story of Paul in Athens, did you notice that he not only understood why the Greeks worshipped all the idols they did, but he also understood their literature, and, more specifically, their poetry, so that he was able to seamlessly weave all of that into an effective gospel presentation?

Now, the Bible shows that Paul was no dummy. He was a very educated man. And let's be honest—most of us aren't going to be as smart as Paul was. But we still don't have to worry about that for two reasons:

1. We can ask God for wisdom, and He will give it to us. James 1:5 says: "If any of you lacks wisdom, you should ask God, who gives generously to all without finding fault, and it will be given to you" (NIV).
2. God promises that when the time is right, He will tell us what to say. Matthew 10:18-20 says: "Because of me, you will be dragged before rulers and kings to tell them and the Gentiles about your faith. But when someone arrests you, don't worry about what you will say or how you will say it. At that time you will be given the words to say. But you will not really be the one speaking. The Spirit from your Father will tell you what to say."

The apostle Paul brilliantly but simply and effectively explained this concept of sharing and defending the gospel in the letter he wrote to the Christians in the city of Corinth. He basically said this: When it comes to the gospel, we must be all things to all men (see 1 Corinthians 9:19-23). Paul basically said that he didn't want anything—not even himself—to get in the way of sharing and defending the gospel and the Christian faith. It doesn't mean that when you explain it you have to become just like them. Not at all! What it means is that you have to strive to understand them and share and defend the gospel and the faith using words, terms, and concepts that your audience can understand.

Our last point: God will always reward our step of faith with people won to Him. Read Acts 17:32-34. Paul's apologetic received mixed reactions. Some made fun of him, some kept searching for more information, but a few believed. Don't ever hesitate to tell others about Christ because you fear that some will not believe you. God's Word is never wasted and will always pay off in the end (Isaiah 55:10, 11).

People need the good news of Jesus now more than ever. God has placed us on this earth with one purpose: to spread the good news of Jesus Christ to as many people as we possibly can. But many will never see or hear about Jesus unless we share Him. It is not only our responsibility but our privilege to be ambassadors for Christ (see 2 Corinthians 5:20, 21).

Jesus is coming soon, and I want to bring with me as many family members, friends, coworkers, and strangers as I possibly can. I think it's incredible that God loved me enough to die for me, but it's even more incredible that He loves me enough to trust me to share His story with others. He makes us all ambassadors for Him.

Second Peter 3:10-12 says: "The day of the Lord's return will surprise us like a thief. The heavens will disappear with a loud noise, and the heat will melt the whole universe. Then the earth and everything on it will be seen for what they are. Everything will be destroyed. So you should serve and honor God by the way you live. You should look forward to the day when God judges everyone, and you should try to make it come soon."

Now that you've read it, let's get to it. Jesus is coming back, and we can help Him get here sooner!

LIT UP: GLOWING FOR JESUS

In May 2008 I was speaking at a conference. Usually I try to take my family on as many speaking engagements as I can for two reasons:

1. When my wife and I got married, I promised her a family vacation at least once a year. And for the most part, I've been true to my word.

2. My wife stays home and raises our two children, and I've come to this conclusion: regular family vacations are much easier on the wallet than weekly therapy sessions or a weekly visit to the spa—or both!

Anyhow, I was doing only one presentation, so we were spending three nights in Chattanooga, Tennessee. OK, it's not the most exotic locale, but it's where my wife and I met and fell in love, so it holds a lot of fond memories. Also, Chattanooga really is a wonderfully fun, family-oriented city.

There was only one problem: The folks who paid me to come there put us up in some "fancy" accommodations. I mean, we had to share a bathroom with only three other people!

The night after I spoke, I was beat, so I went to bed at roughly the same time as the rest of my family. Well, if you're getting older, as I am, preparing for bed sometimes requires a checklist—and apparatuses—rivaling that of a space shuttle crew getting ready for liftoff. There's the toothbrushing with the special toothbrush and toothpaste; then there's the flossing with the special handled flosser dealie (I made that name up); then there's the tongue scraper (unfortunately, I didn't make that one up); then finally there's the mouthwash. And if you're not tired before starting that regimen, then you'll be afterward.

The room was somewhat small, and the sink was not separated by a partition, nor did it have a lovely soft white light. Did I forget to mention that this was a dorm room? Now, I'm sure that it was cleaned thoroughly before we got there, but this was still a dormitory room. Not only could you tell it once you came into the room, but once you entered the hall, you could smell it.

Anyhow, the room actually had two lights: a main light in the center of the room and a light directly over the sink. Many times we just turned on the sink light because it was bright enough to illuminate the entire room—and probably the room next door—and that was cool when everybody was awake. But the next night I stayed awake a couple of hours later in the lobby, doing some research and writing on the computer, so I didn't get to the room until late.

Needless to say, I hadn't planned ahead. If I had planned ahead, I would have brushed my teeth and done all that other stuff right after supper, but as my wife always says to me, "Omar, that'd be too much like right."

So it was well after 11:00 p.m., and my family was snoring—all of them! I wasn't really worried about waking up my daughter; she sleeps like her old man. But my wife and son are extremely light sleepers. I walked into the room and was able to put my books and laptop in the closet by the faint light from the hallway spilling over into the edge of the room, but there was no way that I was going to be able to get changed into my pajamas.

So there I was, standing in the pitch-black, trying to figure out what to do. I started to pray hard. Then I had a thought, and it was too smart to come from me, so I thanked God and pulled out my cell phone. If any of you have been to a concert lately, you know what I'm about to do. I gently opened the phone (remember, the room was pitch-black), I punched a key, and it made a loud beeping sound. My son shifted in his bed, and I held my breath. Remembering my ninja training, I slowed my breathing, calmed my heartbeat, and became very still. I waited a little bit, turned off the sound, and tried again.

This time I pressed the key, and presto! The phone lit up the entire room. The light from my teeny little cell phone was so bright that I had to cover it with my hand. I quickly took off my white T-shirt and wrapped my cell phone in it. This dimmed the light somewhat, but still gave me enough light to get everything done. As I pulled the covers over me, the Holy Spirit impressed upon my mind two incredibly deep spiritual truths about this situation:

1. The more pervasive the darkness is, the brighter a light—any light, even a small one—will be upon that darkness.
2. The moment I stopped pressing the buttons on my phone, the light went off and the room got dark again! For there to be light, I had to be actively doing something to give off that light.

And then in a flash the Holy Spirit (I can always tell when the Holy Spirit is working, because I don't do anything in a flash except for put my foot in my mouth) brought two passages of Scripture to my mind:

"You are the light of the world. A town built on a hill cannot be hidden. Neither do people light a lamp and put it under a bowl. Instead they put it on its stand, and it gives light to everyone in the house" (Matthew 5:14, 15, NIV).

"Do everything without grumbling or arguing, so that you may become blameless and pure, 'children of God without fault in a warped and crooked generation.' Then you will shine among them like stars in the sky as you hold firmly to the word of life" (Philippians 2:14-16, NIV).

As I pondered these two incredible truths, I began to think about my life and how many times I've "hid" my light because I was afraid of not knowing what to say or being rejected by others. But then I thought about a sadder truth: How many more times have I told others about Jesus, but dimmed my "light" by wrapping it up in the "T-shirts" of worldliness, watering down truth so as not to offend or upset anybody?

In the end, not sharing Jesus or changing the truth to make it easier to swallow are both unacceptable to God. He wants us to be bold—not rude, but honest, clear, and concise. It's not hard to do. In fact, if you have a daily, real relationship with Jesus, then it should be easy.

I find it very easy to brag on my wife and talk all about her wonderful qualities. In fact, my wife jokingly states, "Omar, you talk about me as if I walk on water!" And I do, because I love and adore my wife. Do you have that kind of relationship with Jesus? I certainly hope so.

When you tell your story as a Christian, here are three steps that should help you:

1. Start with talking about your life before you accepted Christ.
2. Then talk about how you accepted Christ.
3. End with talking about your life now, after you accepted Christ.

Also, here are three things to keep in mind when you tell your story:

1. Listen to the Holy Spirit.
2. Be real and honest.
3. Be ready for results.

Paul's testimony found in Acts 22:1-22 illustrates my points beautifully. Give it a read right now. Here's some background: Paul is set on going to Jerusalem, but he's warned by many people in many cities and in many ways about what will happen to him when he goes to Jerusalem. But Paul insists. Paul basically says that whether he lives or dies is not the point, because he is ready to die for Jesus.

So Paul goes to Jerusalem. Paul arrives in Jerusalem and starts a riot. (Everywhere Paul goes he's starting a riot, because he refuses to water down the gospel message.) There's a definite lesson here. How many people get upset when you talk about your relationship with God? Or do you avoid talking about it at all costs?

As he was warned, Paul gets arrested, but he asks to speak to the crowd trying to kill him. Are you catching this? Paul isn't concerned about himself. He sees this as a chance to preach to the folk who are looking to hurt him. Talk about devotion! So Paul tells his story.

Paul is honest. He doesn't pull any punches. He shares candidly about his crazy life and his "baggage." But—more important—he also shares how he met Christ and about the power of Jesus in his life. Every time a person does this, there's always a response (sometimes good, sometimes bad). What I've found is that when you share the gospel honestly and with power, people's hearts will either melt or harden.

Sometimes they'll open up and tell you their story, or sometimes they'll become overwhelmingly angry. Don't get a big head if they accept Christ. It's not you; it's Christ working through you. Conversely, if they get angry, remember that you're just the messenger. Yeah, it's a drag, but sometimes when you represent somebody, you end up catching a lot of flak that's intended for them. In this case, people may feel upset because you're raining on their parade.

The Bible calls the Ten Commandments a mirror. If you have a mess on your face, sleep in your eyes, and cornflakes in your hair when you look in the mirror, you're going to see the dirt and the mess. The mirror reflects the reality. When you see that stuff, you can either clean it off or break the mirror and go on living with your messy face. In a way, you are that mirror for the world. Paul calls us Christ's ambassadors and living letters. People may never set foot in a church or read a Bible, but they've got to see Christ when they come in contact with you.

When you share your testimony about what you've seen, heard, and experienced, both before and after knowing Christ, you are a first-person witness. That's why Christians call the act of telling their story "witnessing." You can't give your testimony if you haven't witnessed Christ.

Now that I'm done talking about theory, let's put it into real-life application. I've got an assignment for you. First, write your testimony; then give it to a Christian. Let them give you some constructive criticism. You can then make changes and start to pray the "Three Openings Prayer": "God, open an opportunity for me to share my testimony, open someone's heart to your Holy Spirit, and finally, open my mouth and give me the boldness and courage to share the lifesaving and life-changing message with somebody else."

HOW NOT TO BE A FOOL (LIVING LIFE WISELY)

Son, I'm so glad you graduated today," exclaimed my father as he wiped away tears of joy and then bear-hugged me. He hesitated, sighing deeply; I could tell that he was working hard to fight back more tears.

I remember thinking: *What deep words of knowledge and fatherly wisdom will he give to me?*

My dad then put his hands on my shoulders and made sure that he had my full attention. He took another deep breath and said words that will stick with me until I die. "Son, I thought you were stupid!" Then he flicked a quarter at me and gruffly said, "Now, buy a paper and get a job!"

I am not lying. These are the words he told me as I was graduating—from eighth grade!

Growing up, I was a fool. My father used to tell me that my head was made of granite, because I was hardheaded. I got a lot of spankings because I did a lot of stupid things that made problems for me at school, at home, and pretty much everywhere. I was, as I said, a fool.

In this chapter we'll explore what the Bible has to say about being a "fool," or, more specifically, about not being a fool. We'll be asking and answering some key questions:

1. What is wisdom? What is the value of wisdom for my life?
2. What is the difference between knowledge and wisdom?
3. Is there anybody who has already made big mistakes, learned from them, and written this stuff down for others to learn from?
4. What is the book of Proverbs?
5. What is a proverb? Who wrote the book of Proverbs?
6. What is the purpose of the proverbs?
7. What are the key themes of Proverbs?
8. What can we learn and apply to our own lives about how Solomon answered God's "most important question"?

First, what is wisdom, and why should I care? Plainly put, wisdom is the ability to live in an intelligent and good way. Now, I'm no egghead—although I really wish I were. But Mr. Webster, the dictionary guy (and definitely an egghead), uses words such as these to define wisdom: the "ability to discern inner qualities and relationships"; "insight"; "good sense." So basically, wisdom is the ability to have good insight, good sense, common sense (it's not so common these days), and good judgment to make good decisions.

So now that we know what wisdom is, what is the value of wisdom—and how can we get wisdom for ourselves? I've talked to a lot of teens in my short years, and typically teens answer the question "Can you have wisdom for yourself?" something like this: "Well, I'm really not old enough to have a lot of wisdom yet. Maybe when I get older, I'll have some."

A lot of teens think that getting wisdom is like getting money: when they get older, they'll be able to save up for their retirement. We all tend to think that the only people who have wisdom live in nursing homes or up in some mountain hideaway.

Not quite. The Bible tells us something different: It promises us that "if any of you lack wisdom, you should pray to God, who will give it to you; because God gives generously and graciously to all" (James 1:5, TEV).

Wisdom is knowing where or when to apply knowledge correctly. You would think that this would be extremely useful. If so, then why don't more people have wisdom? Well, the bottom line is because it comes at a price. That price is your pride. Getting wisdom begins with the understanding that you aren't smart enough to get it yourself. It comes from God, and you need to go to Him to get it. The Bible teaches that if you want wisdom, you've got to respect and obey the Lord. Proverbs 9:10 says: "The fear of the Lord is the beginning of wisdom" (NIV).

Fear? Fearing the Lord is entirely different from being fearful or afraid of Him. Fearing the Lord means that you understand that there is only one God in the universe and that you are not Him. Once you understand that simple point, you are well on your way to having wisdom.

The next logical question is: How do you know if you fear the Lord? Easy: respect for somebody is ultimately measured in obedience. Do you obey God even when it goes against what you want to do? when it will cost you something that is dear to you? That's when you truly know that you fear God. When you're willing to give all for Him and still follow Him, that's when you know that you fear Him.

In the Old Testament book of Job, God says of Job: "There is no one on earth like him; he is blameless and upright, a man who fears God and shuns evil" (Job 1:8, NIV). Now pay attention to Job's attitude after he's lost his earthly possessions and all his family but his wife. He says, "The Lord gave and the Lord has taken away; may the name of the Lord be praised" (Job 1:21, NIV). Later, even after losing his health, Job says of God: "Though he slay me, yet will I hope in him" (Job 13:15, NIV).

What? Job just lost everything, and he's praising God? Job reiterates that his focus is God and God alone. *Wow*—to have faith and obedience to God truly puts you in an incredibly submissive position so that He can use you. That's why it matters so much to understand who God really is. You can't expect to get anything coming down the pipeline from God if you don't even believe that He is the one who alone can give it!

Let's review. If you want wisdom, whom do you have to ask? Not Socrates, not Aristotle, not Plato, not Albert Einstein, not the Dalai Lama, not Bill Gates, not Dr. Phil, not Oprah—not even Ellen White. The only being in the entire universe who has it to give away is God! Never forget that.

You may say to yourself, "I've got lots of knowledge. I mean, I know lots of stuff." But knowledge is not wisdom. Knowledge is information, or "book learning," but wisdom is effectively, happily, and successfully living life. Wisdom is the proper application of the right knowledge.

Now that you know the difference between the two, which one do you have: knowledge or wisdom? As we said before, if you don't have wisdom, you can ask God for it, and He promises to give it to you.

I'm sure there have been times in your life when you may have said, "Wow, I wish there was someone who could guide me through life and set me on the right path to live a healthy, happy, and successful life." A lot of the teens I've seen with serious negative life issues have consistently refused to listen to other people who know more, have lived longer, have made bigger mistakes, and have learned from them. The Bible calls this type of people who refuse to listen fools.

Many teens tend to listen to and then do the things that people their own age tell them to—people who have little to no real-life experience; people who are in the process of making big, serious, bad life mistakes or are already experiencing the negative consequences of those mistakes; or people who don't seem to learn from their mistakes! This is what I like to call the jailhouse lawyer phenomenon. Let me explain: There are lots of "experts" on the law in jail, and if you're in there talking with them, they've got a bazillion ideas and theories about how to get out of jail—*but they're in jail!*

How about talking to people who have made bad decisions and have learned from them enough to keep them from going to jail, or people who have been in jail but have gotten out and not headed back? Those are the people you need to listen to.

Well, thank God that there was someone who was a bigger fool than you or me or any of your friends. His name was Solomon, and he was a king. I know, I know. Just because you're a king doesn't mean you won't make stupid life decisions. In the book of Ecclesiastes he lists all the stupid stuff he did trying to find fulfillment in everything else but God. Then in the book of Proverbs Solomon gives the "cheat sheet," or short version, of the most important things he learned about living a godly life and having happiness, joy, impact, peace, purpose, and power.

King Solomon was known as the wisest man in the world. The Bible states that there has never been—nor will there ever be—anyone wiser than Solomon. Solomon composed 3,000 proverbs and 1,005 songs; however, only about 800 of his 3,000 proverbs are included in the book of Proverbs. He wrote the Song of Solomon, Proverbs, and Ecclesiastes—three of the four "wisdom" books in the Bible. That fact alone should send up a red flag that we should be listening to him!

So what is a proverb? It's a short, concise sentence that conveys moral truth. The word "proverb" comes from the Hebrew word that can mean "to rule or to govern," and these sayings, reminders, and warnings provide profound advice for governing our lives. Proverbs is broken down into three different sections:

1. Wisdom for young people (chapters 1-9)
2. Wisdom for all people (chapters 10-24)
3. Wisdom for leaders (chapters 25-31)

I find it interesting that Solomon wrote proverbs to teenagers first. All the proverbs are important, but of crucial importance are the first ones that deal with the issues that historically have messed up teens' lives: not listening to parents, hanging out with the wrong crowd, and sex! Teens, get a clue: read and pore over these proverbs. Let them soak into your life, your beliefs, and your behavior, because if you do, you really will make it out of your teen years able to live a better, happier, and longer life!

So what is the purpose of Proverbs? Well, Solomon, being the brainiac that he was, actually included an introduction to explain what he was going to talk about and why it was important. It's found in Proverbs 1:1-7: "These are the proverbs of King Solomon of Israel, the son of David. Proverbs will teach you wisdom and self-control and how to understand sayings with deep meanings. You will learn what is right and honest and fair. From these, an ordinary person can learn to be smart, and young people can gain knowledge and good sense. If you are already wise, you will become even wiser. And if you are smart, you will learn to understand proverbs and sayings, as well as words of wisdom and all kinds of riddles. Respect and obey the Lord! This is the beginning of knowledge. Only a fool rejects wisdom and good advice."

Now that we know the purpose of the book of Proverbs, let's discover the key themes of chapters 1 to 9. Following the introduction, there is a series of warnings, bits of advice, or words of encouragement, each beginning with "my son." These messages introduce the concept of wisdom in the format of a father's efforts to persuade his son to pursue the path of wisdom in order to achieve godly success in life.

- Wisdom rejects the invitation of crime and foolishness.
- Wisdom rewards seekers of wisdom on every level.
- Wisdom provides freedom and safety (chapters 1 to 4).
- Wisdom protects one from illegitimate sensuality and its consequences.
- Wisdom protects one from foolish practices and laziness.
- Wisdom protects one from adultery and the lure of the whore/prostitute (chapters 5 to 7).
- Wisdom is to be preferred to silliness or foolishness because of its divine origin and rich benefits (chapters 8 and 9).

The book of Proverbs speaks strongly and specifically about fools. There are four kinds of fools, ranging from those who are naive and uncommitted to scoffers who arrogantly despise the way of God. Basically, a scoffer is someone who makes fun of somebody else. The fool is not someone who is mentally deficient, stupid, or mentally retarded; instead, the Bible's definition of a fool is someone who consistently chooses as a pattern of their character to remain ignorant and/or doesn't receive or accept wise advice and lives as though there is no God.

Basically, a fool is someone who thinks they know more than everybody else, and they don't listen to anybody's advice. A fool is somebody who thinks they won't get into trouble or bad things won't happen to them. A fool thinks that all those consequences will happen to somebody else, and even when they get into trouble or suffer consequences, they refuse to listen and learn from their mistakes. Typically a fool likes to play the blame game, shift responsibility, make excuses, or just plain lie about stuff!

I've got a few questions for you: Are you a fool? Do you know somebody in your family who's a fool? Are you friends with a fool? If you're a fool, stop it. Speaking from much life experience, I can tell you: it won't get you anywhere. If you know somebody who's a fool, warn them lovingly and strongly that bad and difficult things are coming down the road for them—and they won't be able to avoid them.

I want to finish up this chapter by discussing the three benefits of wisdom. I also want us to look at how we would respond if God gave us a blank check. As you read about these benefits, think about yourself and the people you know and love. Do any of the things about being a fool describe you or anybody you know? If so, you can begin to make appropriate changes in your life. Remember what God says about your behavior: your choices affect your consequences. Smart choices = good consequences; stupid choices = bad consequences. It's all up to you.

The Bible calls King Solomon the wisest man in the world. In fact, it says that there was never anyone like him, nor will there ever be anyone like him. If you read, study, and take to heart the information that Solomon gives you in Proverbs and surround yourself with wise and not foolish people, you'll make smart choices.

So what are the benefits of wisdom?

A. *Long life and good health.* Proverbs 8:35, 36 tells us: "By finding me [Wisdom], you find life, and the Lord will be pleased with you. But if you don't find me, you hurt only yourself, and if you hate me, you are in love with death." More examples are found in Proverbs 1:32, 33; 3:1-3; 3:15-18; 3:21, 22; 4:10; 4:22.

B. *The ability to choose friends wisely.* Proverbs 1:8-19 states: "My child, obey the teachings of your parents, and wear their teachings as you would a lovely hat or a pretty necklace. Don't be tempted by sinners or listen when they say, 'Come on! Let's gang up and kill somebody, just for the fun of it! They're well and healthy now, but we'll finish them off once and for all. We'll take their valuables and fill our homes with stolen goods. If you join our gang, you'll get your share.' Don't follow anyone like that or do what they do. They are in a big hurry to commit some crime, perhaps even murder. They are like a bird that sees the bait, but ignores the trap. They gang up to murder someone, but they are the victims. The wealth you get from crime robs you of your life." More examples are found in Proverbs 2:12-15.

C. *Safety from ungodly sexuality.* Proverbs 2:16-19 states: "Wisdom will protect you from the smooth talk of a sinful woman, who breaks her wedding vows and leaves the man she married when she was young. The road to her house leads down to the dark world of the dead. Visit her, and you will never find the road to life again." More examples are found in Proverbs 5:1-23; 6:20-35; 7.

What would you do if someone handed you a blank check and said that you can buy whatever you want—the sky's the limit? There are no restrictions, and you can have anything your heart desires! Well, we're going to look at a story of someone who got just that—from God! It's found in 1 Kings 3:1-15. Read the story in whatever version you like.

Now let's discuss eight important lessons that we need to learn from Solomon on the importance of wisdom and how to get it from God:

1. Solomon showed his love for the Lord by recognizing God as the Creator and sustainer of all things. Solomon also kept God's laws and commandments (see verse 3). How about you? Do you recognize that God is the boss? If you do, are you living a life that reflects that fact?
2. Solomon worshipped God without end (see verses 3, 4). He offered 1,000 burnt offerings to God. Can you imagine the blood—and the smell? What about you? What are you giving to God for your worship? How are you sacrificing to God? What gifts of your life, time, money, and talents are you giving to Him?
3. Solomon had the right viewpoint of who he was in front of God (see verses 6-8). Solomon would become the richest, smartest, and most powerful person in the whole world, but when he spoke to God, he called himself "your servant" and a "little child." It's uncomfortable for us to humble ourselves. But I'd rather do it willingly than have God do it for me. How about you? For more on this, see the story of King Nebuchadnezzar in Daniel 4. Interesting stuff, but definitely not a lesson you would want to learn the hard way.

Solomon admitted that he could do nothing by himself. Again, Solomon humbled himself and reminded himself that God was God. He admitted his weaknesses by telling God the truth. He was feeling incredibly overwhelmed, but the key was that he admitted it. He told God that he didn't know how to carry out his duties and that the people he was going to rule were too many to count (1 Kings 3:7, 8). You see, the key is humility and a teachable spirit. In fact, as you'll learn, the Bible takes a dim view of people who are prideful, who always think they're right and can't or won't take guidance or advice from others. The Bible calls them fools! Just so we're clear, that's bad and the opposite of someone who is wise.

4. Solomon prioritized his life properly. He asked God for a discerning heart so he could help his people (verse 9). Solomon's motivations were right and unselfish. I would probably have asked for a discerning heart so that I could make better decisions on how to trade my money in the stock market. You know what I mean? It would have all been for me!

5. God was pleased and gave Solomon his request (verses 10-12). We've already read in the book of James that God will grant our request for wisdom if we just ask and believe that He will grant it. But the key is that we have to have the right attitude and motivations. God's not going to give you wisdom just so you can be selfish.
6. Furthermore, because Solomon's motives were right, God blessed him with everything else (verse 13). He blessed Solomon with all the stuff that he had not asked for. Specifically, the Bible tells us that he was blessed with riches and honor.

Now, I want to be careful here. I'm not saying that if you choose to worship and fear God, He will make you rich and important—not at all! Sometimes God chooses to give incredibly great material things as a consequence of someone's faith, but many times He does not. But God will always give us what we need in this life—and more important, in the life to come. "I tell you not to worry about your life. Don't worry about having something to eat, drink, or wear. Isn't life more than food or clothing? Look at the birds in the sky! They don't plant or harvest. They don't even store grain in barns. Yet your Father in heaven takes care of them. Aren't you worth more than birds?" (Matthew 6:25, 26). "Don't worry and ask yourselves, 'Will we have anything to eat? Will we have anything to drink? Will we have any clothes to wear?' Only people who don't know God are always worrying about such things. Your Father in heaven knows that you need all of these. But more than anything else, put God's work first and do what he wants. Then the other things will be yours as well" (verses 31-33).

7. If you stay on God's side, He will give you a long and happy life (1 Kings 3:14). If you read the first nine chapters of Proverbs—remember, they're written for you—you will see this theme again and again. God wants you to live a long, happy, and prosperous life, and the only way you can do that is to be on His side.
8. Even in his success, Solomon didn't forget where he came from, and praised and thanked God for His goodness and blessings (verse 15). It would have been easy for Solomon to take credit for his wisdom and forget God. And Solomon did just that for a long time—the Bible honestly records Solomon's mistakes as a warning to us. But thank God that near the end of Solomon's life he recognized his serious mistakes and came running back to God!

I hope that it won't take you almost your entire life to come back to God. Turn to Him today. You will indeed be turning from death to life.

Solomon and the other writers of Proverbs knew that the teen years are the most difficult for many, and during this time you will make some of the most important decisions of your life, many of which may fundamentally change your life—either positively or negatively.

In light of Proverbs, closely examine your life, your habits, your choices, and your relationships with your friends and "special" friends. Take the truths expressed in the first nine chapters—and in the rest of the book of Proverbs—to heart and make changes where you need to. That way you won't get caught up in something that you can't get out of and you can be free to fully give your physical, emotional, and spiritual strength to serving God and speeding His return to take us all home!

YOUR REPLACEMENT IS HERE!

I knew it was coming: we're being replaced! I'll give you the highlights of the interesting (and disturbing) story I just read. I think the title says it all: "Teens Take Celebrity Cutouts as Prom Dates: Darling or Disturbing?"*

The author speaks about a Colorado teen who just had to have Justin Bieber as her prom date. When she wasn't able to get the real Bieber, she took a life-size cardboard cutout of him. The two had a great time—dancing, having professional pictures taken—and the girl says she wasn't upset by any weird looks that came her way.

The author mentions another teen who did just about the same thing the very same week in Iowa, only with a Tim Tebow cutout as her date.

"The fad might not be so funny if it continues to gain momentum," we read later in the article. The author quotes a psychotherapist—Dr. Nancy Irwin—as saying, "Having a cardboard cutout in your bedroom can be OK, but to simulate a date or 'real' relationship in a public place is disallowing for real flesh-and-blood humans—who are not airbrushed—to interact with you."

Dr. Irwin did go on to say, "If it were a special event, a singular 'theme party,' it would be healthy, but to replace a human being, especially one that is idolized—as celebrities are—is making a statement that your peers are not good enough for you."

Did you catch what was going on? A teen was so rabid with Bieber fever that she took a cutout of the star to the prom! I absolutely agree with the psychotherapist: this sends a dangerous and creepy kind of statement. And that statement is clear: If I don't like my options for real, flesh-and-blood people, I'll just take care of my needs myself and make my own!

This isn't just an interesting or disturbing story; it's also an important reminder that as teens and Christians, it's crucial that you learn to focus on what is real and eternal. The Bible tells us that we should focus our minds and attention on the things of heaven, not on what's on this earth. This article simply illustrates the power, influence, and importance of both stardom and our want-it, need-it, get-it-*now* culture.

Hollywood blockbuster movies such as *Avatar* and *Gamer* (tagline: "Who's playing you?") and the rising popularity of role-playing video games clearly illustrate our culture's postmodern mentality that believes that truth is created rather than found, and if you don't like something, well, just change it; after all, you're in control of your life. Here's the bottom line: If we choose to focus our mind and attention on this type of thinking, we'll for sure be transformed, and not in a good way!

The Bible clearly states in 1 John 2:15-17: "Don't love the world or anything that belongs to the world. If you love the world, you cannot love the Father. Our foolish pride comes from this world, and so do our selfish desires and our desire to have everything we see. None of this comes from the Father. The world and the desires it causes are disappearing. But if we obey God, we will live forever."

You see, as Christians we cannot love both the world and God. Being a Christian is an "either-or" choice. It's not multiple choice. God is looking for teens who as Christians don't act like everybody else but are truly different. The apostle Paul told the Romans, who were living in a culture that was very much like our own today: "Dear friends, God is good. So I beg you to offer your bodies to him as a living sacrifice, pure and pleasing. That's the most sensible way to serve God. Don't be like the people of this world, but let God change the way you think. Then you will know how to do everything that is good and pleasing to him" (Romans 12:1, 2).

Things won't always be perfect for us as Christians living in this world. But we don't need to fear. God has said that He will never leave us or forsake us. Jesus told His disciples: "While you are in the world, you will have to suffer. But cheer up! I have defeated the world" (John 16:33).

While we're going through this life, it's 100 percent guaranteed that we'll have problems. But as Christians we need to be doing things differently and have our minds focused on things that are eternal. For we know that our home is ultimately not on this earth, and when we get to heaven, the real party's going to start.

Jesus, reassuring His disciples about all the loss and suffering they would experience as His followers, spoke these awesome words that are valid for us as well: "Yes, all of you have become my followers. And so in the future world, when the Son of Man sits on his glorious throne, I promise that you will sit on twelve thrones to judge the twelve tribes of Israel. All who have given up home or brothers and sisters or father and mother or children or land for me will be given a hundred times as much. They will also have eternal life. But many who are now first will be last, and many who are last will be first" (Matthew 19:28-30).

Why is it important for us as Christians to recognize and embrace these truths? Because if we're not sold on these truths, then how will we be able to first live them out and second tell others about them? Let me ask you a question: How well do you believe and live out these truths? Is there a difference between what you believe and how you behave? Do you need to make changes in your life? If you do, what are they? Whom do you need to get to help you make those changes and keep those changes up?

I want to encourage you to think clearly about your life, your view of truth, and how it affects your interactions with others in this world. As Christians we want to hold out the Word of truth to non-Christians and let them drink from Jesus the life-giving water that totally quenches and satisfies their thirst for what they can't get from others and the world.

---

*www.foxnews.com/entertainment/2012/05/08/teens-take-celebrity-cut-outs-as-prom-dates-darling-or-disturbing

IS THERE ANYONE LIKE ME OUT THERE?

Here's a post from the *Insight* discussion board that caught my attention:

OK, so I'm not your average teen. I hate fads and fashion and anything to do with relationships, teenage drama—anything teenagerish. Instead, I'm into medical science. I love to study and learn about the human body, and

about all the different kinds of diseases and disorders. My friends and cousins all think I'm really weird and kind of "brainy" because I'm always telling them interesting human body facts. And anytime one of my friends comes to tell me about anything teenagerish, I'm not interested. So I was just wondering, is there anyone like me out there? Sometimes I feel so alone, as if I'm the only one who is so different from all the teens my age.—Amanda.

Amanda, I'm so glad that you posted this question/concern. As a counselor for many years, I've dealt with tons of teens with that same concern: just because they're different from everybody else—with unique skills, interests, and talents—are they somehow weird or bad? There is nothing wrong with you; you're functioning the exact way that God made you to function.

God made you the way you are for a purpose. Have you ever thought that maybe God wants you to go into the medical sciences? Hidden deep within your brain may be the cure for cancer or AIDS, or maybe you'll discover a way to rebuild human organs or another incredible way to help humanity! Albert Einstein was different from all his family and playmates as a child, teen, and young adult, but look at what he accomplished.

I get the feeling that you've been receiving a lot of comments and possibly some bullying. But again I say that God made you just the way you're supposed to be. In fact, God has given you a unique mix of spiritual gifts, a specific recipe of things that you're interested in and things you're good at that are as unique as your fingerprints.

The Bible talks in many places about spiritual gifts, but the three main passages are in Romans 12, 1 Corinthians 12, and Ephesians 4. Space is limited, so you can just read the lists for yourself, but I will mention a couple of things in general about spiritual gifts:

- There are different kinds of spiritual gifts, but they all come from God (1 Corinthians 12:4, 5).
- Each person should use whatever gift(s) they have received to serve others, and they should use them consistently and responsibly and not waste them (1 Peter 4:10).
- Everybody in God's family is made to do something different and unique (Romans 12:4-6).
- Jesus tells us that if you don't use your spiritual gifts, you will lose them (Matthew 25:14-28).

So now that you know this about yourself, what's the next step? First, you need to be OK with who you are, and that starts with an understanding that "God made you special and He loves you very much!" (I took that from the VeggieTales gang—simple, but deep!)

Second, you should do some reading about spiritual gifts. There are tons of resources about this on the Internet, but I would encourage you to contact your local youth pastor or youth group teacher. Then you need to educate your friends and family about your spiritual gifts and also let them know about theirs.

Third, you've got to plug into your church and begin using your gifts. God doesn't want you to be a blessing just to the church, though. He also wants you to use that same unique mix to bless people outside of the church as well. Many teens find that their spiritual gifts translate into secular career choices, and many times those fit together great. Why is that? Well, if you enjoy something and are good at it, then it doesn't seem like work to you.

Last, you've got to continue working to improve and refine your spiritual gifts. This likely means education, education, and more education. But it doesn't always mean sitting-in-a-classroom education. You may be interested in "job shadowing" someone who is a medical professional or interviewing someone who is doing something that you're interested in, or maybe even spending several weeks or months interning (working for free to get the experience) at a company.

Remember, now is the time for you to invest in yourself and educate your brain for God. Imagine trying to dig a hole with a spoon and then how much more awesome it would be to have one of those big, powerful, earthmoving machines with a big scoop on it. That's the picture of you trying to help others without an education; sure, you could do it with a spoon, but how much better would it be with a "big scoop" education?

Amanda, never be afraid or embarrassed about who you are and who God made you to be. God made you awesome—so be awesome! David wrote these powerful words:

"You [God] are the one who put me together inside my mother's body, and I praise you because of the wonderful way you created me. Everything you do is marvelous! Of this I have no doubt. Nothing about me is hidden from you! I was secretly woven together deep in the earth below, but with your own eyes you saw my body being formed. Even before I was born, you had written in your book everything I would do" (Psalm 139:13-16).

Don't worry what everybody else thinks about you. The one person whose opinion ultimately matters is God . . . and He thinks you're pretty great.

THE SECRET TO CONTENTMENT

"I can do all things, all things, all things, I can do all things through Christ who strengthens me," sang my daughter while jumping up and down with her eyes closed, swinging her pink and purple pom-poms in my face.

When she finished, her mother and I exploded into applause and general parent mayhem. The text she was singing, Philippians 4:13, NKJV, is good news in itself, but when read within the larger context of the passage it's in—well, it's even better news.

What's the context, you ask? We'll get to it in a little bit. Don't get ahead of the story!

Several years ago my daughter and I began to memorize Bible texts that were important to us. Philippians 4:13 was the second one she memorized; the first was John 3:16. I know that you just said the verse to yourself as soon as you read this. I love playing with your heads!

I find it interesting that teenagers—at least in this country—have a difficult time being satisfied or contented with themselves, the world, the stuff they have—basically everything! It seems that nothing is ever enough for them—and truthfully, it's the same for us adults as well. I just read this post from an anonymous teen with the screen name "han":

"OK, I have loads of silly little problems, but when I look at my life, I'm probably one of the luckiest people in this world. So why am I never fulfilled? I always want something more. I'm just so spoiled. But I have an idea of the perfect life, and I won't accept anything less. I try new things and have fun and all, but what's the point? Sometimes it all feels so pointless. I feel so depressed, but the worst part is knowing that I have absolutely no right to be depressed. I just don't see the point in life. It's not hurtful . . . it's just never-ending boredom."

Do you hear the sheer frustration, boredom, dissatisfaction, depression, and ultimate meaninglessness? I'm sure you have friends who feel the same way. Hey, maybe you feel that way too! So what do you do about it? Is there a solution—something of substance that can fill the hole in our souls? The answer is yes, and you won't be surprised when I tell you. It's . . . you guessed it: Jesus!

Remember I told you about the good news of Philippians 4:13, but there's better news, and it's found in the verses before it and after it. In these verses we'll discover the solutions to (as they say in the South) "what ails ya":

"Not that I was ever in need, for I have learned how to be content with whatever I have. I know how to live on almost nothing or with everything. I have learned the secret of living in every situation, whether it is with a full stomach or empty, with plenty or little. For I can do everything through Christ, who gives me strength. . . . And this same God who takes care of me will supply all your needs from his glorious riches, which have been given to us in Christ Jesus" (verses 11-19, NLT).

Did you catch it? Paul says that the secret to contentment is found in Jesus. That's simple and yet very profound.

You have to understand where Paul was when he was writing this letter. He was in jail! Paul wrote to encourage the Christians of Philippi in their faith during his imprisonment in a Roman prison. In the midst of being in shackles, possibly chained up to other people, without clean water, electricity, Hot Pockets, cable TV, Facebook, the Internet, Wii, or anything else, he wrote that he had learned the secret of being content. Listen, I can understand if you don't want to take my word for it, but if you don't listen to Paul, then I can't help you.

In verse 19 Paul again repeats his main point (for those of us who have ADD): the same God who took care of Paul so long ago can take care of us. Not only can He take care of us, but He is able to supply *all our needs!* Praise God! One of Jesus' disciples named Matthew put it like this: "More than anything else, put God's work first and do what he wants. Then the other things will be yours as well" (Matthew 6:33).

Solomon wrote these deep words: "All of life is far more boring than words could ever say. Our eyes and our ears are never satisfied with what we see and hear. Everything that happens has happened before; nothing is new, nothing under the sun. Someone might say, 'Here is something new!' But it happened before, long before we were born. No one who lived in the past is remembered anymore, and everyone yet to be born will be forgotten too" (Ecclesiastes 1:8-11).

If we are too focused on having things, we can get to the point that we're always looking for the next best, newest, biggest, fastest blah, blah, blah, blah. But in the end, just as Solomon said, we will never be satisfied. But if we focus our attention not on having more stuff but on having more of a relationship with a person (and not just any person—Jesus), then we'll never be disappointed. We'll find that we indeed won't be empty or thirsty, for Jesus said: "Everyone who drinks this water will get thirsty again and again. Anyone who drinks the water I give will never thirst—not ever. The water I give will be an artesian spring within, gushing fountains of endless life" (John 4:13, 14, Message).

I don't know about you, but as the old Southern gospel song says, "I'm drinking from my saucer cause my cup has overflowed." I truly believe that a thankful heart is a contented heart. There is a strong connection between the amount of thankfulness we have in our lives and our level of contentment.

I've been in my share of really difficult situations. Hey, maybe you're in a situation like that right now. Maybe it's a bad relationship or a recent breakup or a difficult class at school. Maybe your parents just got divorced or remarried. Maybe one of your family members or close friends recently died. Or there could be any other number of difficult things that you're dealing with right now. Let's look and see what the Bible has to say about those things.

We'll start in the book of Philippians. Remember, Paul was in jail, writing to the Christians in Philippi. Let's take a look and see if he's complaining:

"Always be glad because of the Lord! I will say it again: Be glad. Always be gentle with others. The Lord will soon be here. Don't worry about anything, but pray about everything. With thankful hearts offer up your prayers and requests to God. Then, because you belong to Christ Jesus, God will bless you with peace that no one can completely understand. And this peace will control the way you think and feel" (Philippians 4:4-7).

Did you catch that? Paul is rotting in prison, and here he's telling other people to be glad and rejoice! He's telling them not to worry about anything, but to pray about everything. And how should they pray? Here's the key: with thankful hearts. Paul is giving us a very important secret to the power of the Christian life, and it's this: God's promises are rock-solid, but many of them are dependent upon us doing something first, as is the case here.

Let's take a look at verses 6 and 7. Paul says that we shouldn't worry about anything, but we should pray about everything. Look at verse 7: "Then . . . God will bless you with peace" that will be an unknown, crazy, out-of-this-world kind of peace! In fact, this peace will be so foreign to others that they won't be able to comprehend why—in the midst of all the crazy you're in the middle of—you're so calm!

Not only will God give you peace, but this peace "will control the way you think and feel." In other words, it'll control your thinking and your emotions. Whoa! By the way, when your friends and family see you going through stressful and difficult things and not cracking under the pressure, they're going to want to know what's up, so you'd better be prepared to answer their questions.

Well, now that we've discussed what to do to be contented, let's briefly discuss the how. Again, a close observation of the text will tell us exactly what to do and how to do it. Look again at verse 6: "Pray about everything. . . . offer up your prayers and requests to God." I like the way *The Amplified Bible* translates the word "petition" as "definite requests"—in other words, we should be as specific as possible with God. The Bible paraphrase *The Message* puts verse 6 like this: "Don't fret or worry. Instead of worrying, pray. Let petitions and praises shape your worries into prayers, letting God know your concerns."

Here's the point: The more worried we are about something, the more specific our prayer requests should be. God doesn't want to hear just your praises or the things you're happy about. God also longs to hear the things you're worried and stressed about.

I don't know about you, but when I have a close relationship with somebody, I don't share just the good stuff that's happening—I also share the bad. That's the power of a close and intimate relationship with somebody.

You can always unload on God. Really! He's waiting for you to. And when you do, I promise that you'll feel better every single time. Why? Because once you do that, you unload your emotional backpack that's been weighing you down and you leave it all at God's feet. And guess what? He's big enough to carry your stuff, and my stuff, and everybody's stuff. What? You mean to tell me that you've never heard the children's song "He's Got the Whole World in His Hands"? Well, I'm changing the lyrics to say "He's got everybody's worries in His hands."

When you open up to God every day, consistently, as a habit, well, let me tell you that after a while you begin to feel lighter, freer, more joyful, more at peace, and more contented with your life and what's happening to you and with you. Being thankful won't make all your problems go away, but it will make Jesus—the problem solver and the perfect peace giver—come closer.

So don't wait another second. Are you stressed out or worried about something? Start talking to Jesus right now. Jesus is just a conversation away. He's ready and willing to listen to the stuff that's going on in your life—all of it.

Now, here's the last secret to contentment, and it's really simple: serve someone else. Our service to others is the truest and surest way that we prove we have a real relationship with Christ (secret 1) and that we are truly thankful (secret 2). The attitude that comes out of a relationship with Christ just can't help ministering to others—as Jesus did—and serving them. Jesus said in Mark 10:45: "For even the Son of Man did not come to be served, but to serve, and to give his life as a ransom for many" (NIV).

Mother Teresa, a world-renowned Catholic nun who spent almost her entire life serving the poorest of the poor in the worst conditions in India, said these wise words about service: "You and I, we are the Church, no? We have to share with our people. Suffering today is because people are hoarding, not giving, not sharing. Jesus made it very clear: Whatever you do to the least of my brethren, you do it to me. Give a glass of water, you give it to me. Receive a little child, you receive me." And I like the clarity of this other quote by her: "Love cannot remain by itself—it has no meaning. Love has to be put into action, and that action is service."

I absolutely agree with what Mother Teresa had to say, and you know what? So did the apostle Paul. He told the Philippians—and us—about how a deep, intimate, and growing relationship with Jesus should be affecting us and how that effect should generate within us a desire to serve others—not just other Christians, but the world at large.

"Christ encourages you, and his love comforts you. God's Spirit unites you, and you are concerned for others. Now make me completely happy! Live in harmony by showing love for each other. Be united in what you think, as if you were only one person. Don't be jealous or proud, but be humble and consider others more important than yourselves. Care about them as much as you care about yourselves and think the same way that Christ Jesus thought: Christ was truly God. But he did not try to remain equal with God. Instead he gave up everything and became a slave, when he became like one of us. Christ was humble. He obeyed God and even died on a cross" (Philippians 2:1-8).

Did you notice how at the beginning Paul is so careful to clearly show a deepening and intimate relationship with Jesus (verse 1), and the natural outgrowth of that relationship is a widening circle of love and concern for others (verses 2-4)? Did you notice that when we spend time with Jesus, we will begin to think like Him, respond like Him, and love like Him (verse 5)? Did you notice the connection there between humility (being humble) and service to others? You and I can never serve anybody if we don't first humble ourselves, and we can't truly have the power—given to us by the Holy Spirit—and the right attitude to humble ourselves if we don't spend time with Jesus.

So it really all begins and ends with Jesus. Paul clearly shows us in verses 5-8 what Jesus did as He humbled Himself to serve us—for more than 30 years! I believe that Paul showed us this for two reasons:

1. So we wouldn't complain about humbling ourselves and would get some perspective.
2. So we would have an example of how we should and could do it.

Now I've got some questions for you to consider that will hopefully end with some concrete action steps to get you to begin and/or possibly increase your service to others:

- Whom can you serve right now? Your family, your friends, your community, your enemies?
- How can you serve? What gifts and talents do you have?
- Where should you serve? Your family, your church, your school, a local charity/community center?
- What should you do? Mentor somebody, answer phones, serve food somewhere?

My hope and prayer is that after you read these words, you'll do the right thing for the right reasons. Doing the right thing for the wrong reasons is still ultimately doing the wrong thing. Just take a look at Matthew 23 and what the religious leaders of Jesus' day did. Jesus says in Matthew 7:24: "Anyone who hears and obeys these teachings of mine is like a wise person who built a house on solid rock."

So don't just read this information and say, "Well, that's good information to know. I guess it's cool for somebody else to do." No! Do something with it, and then do something about it! Remember, Jesus did it for you when you couldn't do it for yourself. Based upon your relationship with Him and your thankful response to His great love and sacrifice for you, serve someone else and keep passing Jesus' love along.

STINKING THINKING

I want to talk about something that plagues a lot of teens: uncontrolled negative, illogical, or irrational thoughts. We don't realize the power that our thoughts have over us. Out of your thoughts flows *everything* else about you. I know I'm sounding like a Jedi knight, but it's true. The Bible states clearly that as someone thinks in their heart, so they are; in other words, our thoughts many times are self-fulfilling: What we think ends up influencing what we do and, ultimately, what we become.

Before we get deeply into this topic, I want to say one thing: a preoccupation with suicidal, self-harming, or consistently depressive or compulsive thoughts should *always* lead you to a trusted adult *immediately*. Don't mess around. If you don't know anyone personally to talk to, several hotlines operate 24/7 with professionals who are there precisely for this purpose. Two organizations to contact are: Substance Abuse and Mental Health Services Administration (SAMHSA) at 1-800-662-4357, and the National Suicide Prevention Lifeline at 1-800-273-8255.

The truth is that lots of people—not just teens—have problems with their thoughts; they just can't stop focusing on negative things. In terms of consistently negative and/or depressive thoughts, no amount of medication can make them think differently. Medications for things such as depression, anxiety, panic attacks, bipolar disorder, and schizophrenia can help people have more energy, motivation, and focus, but ultimately the drugs won't help the habitual pattern of negative, unhealthy, and/or unrealistic thoughts.

Our thoughts become habitual usually in two ways: Either someone is raised in an environment of negativity and unhealthy thought patterns, or they learn it through experiencing some sort of trauma or serious life-altering situation. Or both. The bottom line is this: Either we're made this way by the families we're raised in, or we make ourselves this way by what we experience in the world. Or both.

I've been counseling with teens for a long time, and I've never met a "normal" or perfect family. It doesn't exist. Families are made of individuals, and the Bible tells us that we're all sinful and evil. I know it sounds really depressing, but all is not lost.

There is hope.

There is hope in Jesus, because no matter how unhealthy we have been or what kind of craziness was happening—or *is happening*—in our families, if we're Christians, the Holy Spirit can make us a new creation. The Bible has a lot to say about changing our thoughts and all the benefits that this change will bring us. Look, we all are sinful; there's nothing in any of us that is any good. That's why we've got to plug into an outside source other than ourselves. That's where the Holy Spirit comes into play. Plug and play.

I want to share with you a couple of things, and then I want to end with what the Bible has to say about choosing and controlling our thoughts.

First, repeat after me: "All psychology and counseling is not evil." Go on, say it out loud. Good. Now that we've got that out of the way, let me tell you that much psychology *is* evil. It's evil because it's based upon the idea that human beings are basically good. Many people believe that what the mind can conceive, the mind can achieve, but we already know what the Bible has to say about that. At the same time, as a counselor, I can pair the best of psychology and counseling with what the Bible has to say about stuff and, thus, help the people I work with.

There is a theory of counseling and psychology called cognitive behavioral therapy. This is the type of therapy I like to use because it most closely matches what the Bible has to say about how we think. Here's the bottom line: Fix the way you think, fix the way you act. It's that simple. Well, no, it's not simple at all, but it's possible and very effective. Here's how it works: A = Problem/Event, which leads to B = Thoughts/Core Beliefs, which leads to C = Feelings/Emotions, which ultimately leads to D = Actions/Behaviors.

In other words, when something goes wrong, we tend to already have a predetermined thought or a belief about what that represents to us. These thoughts or core beliefs are formed within us by the family we're raised in or the types of experiences we've had in our lives. These beliefs many times tend to be negative and unrealistic, typically focusing on two larger areas: feeling helpless/powerless and being unworthy or unlovable.

These disordered or unhealthy thoughts and beliefs drive us to feel a certain way—typically not good—that then causes us to act or behave in a specific way. None of this is good. The problem is that many of us believe we can't change anything and thus we are doomed to a lifetime of unhealthy thoughts.

The truth is that we *can* change our thought patterns, and here is where the Holy Spirit comes into play. Let's see what the Bible has to say about this whole matter. Paul writes: "People who are ruled by their desires think only of themselves. Everyone who is ruled by the Holy Spirit thinks about spiritual things. If our minds are ruled by our desires, we will die. But if our minds are ruled by the Spirit, we will have life and peace. Our desires fight against God, because they do not and cannot obey God's laws. If we follow our desires, we cannot please God. You are no longer ruled by your desires, but by God's Spirit, who lives in you. People who don't have the Spirit of

Christ in them don't belong to him. But Christ lives in you. So you are alive because God has accepted you, even though your bodies must die because of your sins. Yet God raised Jesus to life! God's Spirit now lives in you, and he will raise you to life by his Spirit" (Romans 8:5-11).

Paul states in Colossians 3:1-3: "You have been raised to life with Christ. Now set your heart on what is in heaven, where Christ rules at God's right side. Think about what is up there, not about what is here on earth. You died, which means that your life is hidden with Christ, who sits beside God."

In other words, choose to focus only on good things.

Paul says in Philippians 4:8: "Finally, my friends, keep your minds on whatever is true, pure, right, holy, friendly, and proper. Don't ever stop thinking about what is truly worthwhile and worthy of praise."

Paul also says in Philippians 4:6, 7: "Don't worry about anything, but pray about everything. With thankful hearts offer up your prayers and requests to God. Then, because you belong to Christ Jesus, God will bless you with peace that no one can completely understand. And this peace will control the way you think and feel."

Now, here's the kicker: You're probably going to have to do this multiple times a day, because, as I've said before, your thoughts are a product of habit, and you've got to start new habits.

So how do you actually do it? There's a four-step process. The moment you begin to have negative, depressive, anxious, or compulsive thoughts:

1. Pray that God will give you wisdom (James 1:5) to recognize when you're having a negative thought.
2. When you have the thought, immediately stop the thought and pray, giving God your concerns and the things that make you anxious (Philippians 4:6, 7).
3. Examine the thought. Is it positive or negative? What's the unhealthy core belief behind it?
4. Replace the thought with something positive (Philippians 4:8). The Bible tells us that God has only good things in store for us, not bad things (Jeremiah 29:11). The best way that I know to replace negative thoughts with positive ones is to memorize Scripture—both general verses about how much God loves you and specific verses dealing with whatever you're struggling with.

Remember, when you harbor worry and anxious thoughts, you're ultimately not trusting God to care for your needs; that's not a good thing. David said it best in Psalm 119:9-11: "How can a young person stay pure?

By obeying your word. I have tried hard to find you—don't let me wander from your commands. I have hidden your word in my heart, that I might not sin against you" (NLT).

I don't want you to think that just knowing this information will magically change your life overnight. Remember, your negative thoughts didn't happen overnight, so they're not going to change overnight. But every day you and I can make positive choices, take baby steps, and surround ourselves with positive people who love us, who care for us, who will be honest with us, who will hold us accountable, and who will celebrate our achievements. And, if need be, get in touch with a good Christian counselor who can help you.

WHAT'S ON YOUR KEY CHAIN?

I was sitting in the chiropractor's office today waiting to be "snap, crackle, popped!" As I sat there, I began to examine my key chain. Each week I examine something different: one week—the ceiling tiles; another week—the floorboards.

I spent 30 minutes dissecting all the stuff that I had on my key chain. That's when I realized, *Half the keys I've been carrying around for years . . . I don't even need!* Armed with this new information, I did what any sensible person would do—I immediately took them off my key chain . . . for a total of five minutes.

Suddenly I had a feeling of intense, illogical anxiety about this action. As I sat there, I began to frantically make all kinds of excuses about why I couldn't get rid of these keys. On and on went the lame excuses.

Truth be told, within five minutes those same keys I had scrutinized and examined were back on my key chain. Why? Simply because I wasn't ready to let go of what they represented in the past. All those keys represented how I perceived myself—good or bad. I wanted to hold on to them because I was comfortable with the way they made me feel about me. Healthy or unhealthy, I had been carrying these keys for a long time, and they were now part of me.

I'm happy to let you know that at that point God decided to enter the conversation. He quickly let me know that I was being ridiculous. He reminded me who I was in Him and literally told me, "Omar, let the keys go!" In the end I found the nearest trash can, and now those extra keys live there. I can't describe the incredible joy and peace that I received by obeying God and letting go of something that was holding me down and keeping me from being all that I could be.

This incident made me think deeply about the things that we decide to hold on to in our lives: things—both good and bad—we think are too important to give to God, yet all the while they're causing us untold stress, anxiety, or pride. It might be stuff that we've been holding on to that mattered to us or made us feel good about ourselves at some point in our past, but now, in the light of a relationship with Jesus, these things are absolutely useless and worthless (see Philippians 3:1-11).

How do we just let go of all the stuff from our past, some of it small, some of it big, but all of it weighing us down and holding us back? Simply put, we change our focus from ourselves to Jesus. The apostle Paul writes: "I have not yet reached my goal, and I am not perfect. But Christ has taken hold of me. So I keep on running and struggling to take hold of the prize. My friends, I don't feel that I have already arrived. But I forget what is behind, and I struggle for what is ahead. I run toward the goal, so that I can win the prize of being called to heaven" (Philippians 3:12-14).

I know there are only three verses there, but like Christmas fruitcake, they're dense! Let's unpack what he's saying and see how we can apply it to our lives.

Just a reminder: Paul was a *psycho!* Before he became Paul, he was Saul. His résumé read: "Super-Jew! A perfect Pharisee! In charge of hunting down Christians, torturing them, and imprisoning and killing them." That was his identity. It was who he was, and he was good at it. So if you think you've got a painful past that causes you emotional pain, guilt, hurt, and shame, Paul's got you beat.

The first part of the process is to be honest about our level of spiritual maturity (verse 12). Paul recognizes that although he's better than he used to be, he's not yet where he needs to be. Second, Paul recognizes that it's God who's initiated this positive change in him (verse 12). Third, he's persistent and active. Look at the words he uses in the second part of verse 12: "running and struggling."

Then in verse 13 and the first part of verse 14, he clarifies the process of running and struggling even more by stating that he has to actively "forget what is behind" and "struggle for what is ahead." This means that daily he has to reprogram his mind and his thoughts on Jesus and what's truly important.

Last, he completes this process by always keeping the goal in front of him. Verse 14 begins: "I run toward the goal." What's the "goal" and "prize" that he mentions three times in these verses? Well, in verse 14 he tells us that it's heaven. Paul understands that as long as we're on this earth, we'll constantly be struggling to be all that we can be.

But if we stay on that road, one day, like Paul, we will be able to say that we have finished the race, we have kept the faith, and we are ready to see God (see 2 Timothy 4:6-8).

FIVE CONCLUSIONS

Now that we've taken a whirlwind tour of Solomon's life through answering a lot of your questions and sharing a lot of my experiences, we'll end up exactly where we started . . . with the question that Solomon asked and answered. Let's see what the wisest man in history ultimately realized.

His conclusions are found in Ecclesiastes 11:7-12. Take a minute and read them for yourself. I promise that it will be some of the most important time you've ever spent.

The first conclusion that Solomon came to was that we're all going to die. Solomon wisely concluded that death is certain for all of us. Some have called death the "ultimate equalizer." I've dealt with a lot of teenagers in my life, and teenagers seem to have this idea that they'll live forever and that they're invincible—until someone they know dies.

Wise and foolish, rich and poor—in the end, we all end up dead. This knowledge is what led Solomon to the second conclusion (which is appropriate for us all, but even more timely for you as the reader): Remember your Creator while you are young. A life without God can produce a bitter, lonely, and hopeless old age. A life centered around God is fulfilling; it will make the "days of trouble"—when disabilities, sickness, and handicaps cause barriers to enjoying life—satisfying because of the hope of eternal life.

Being young is exciting. But the excitement of youth can often become a barrier to closeness with God if it makes young people focus on passing pleasures instead of eternal values. Make your strength available to God when it's still yours—during your youthful years. Don't waste it on evil or meaningless activities that become bad habits or addictions and make you bitter and callous. Seek God now!

Solomon's third conclusion is a very serious one. In many ways it should be listed first, because it reveals the key to a life of purpose and joy. Solomon in all his wisdom—and after trying all of his craziness for all of those years—ended up with this gem: fear God.

Really, Solomon? Is that it? This simple rule was worth a lifetime of experiences? Does this sound something like what he wrote in Proverbs 9:10? "The fear of the Lord is the beginning of wisdom" (NKJV). I think Solomon learned his lesson, and he learned it all too well, but at such a high price: a divided kingdom, a personal and family life in ruin, and the majority of his best years wasted. Oh, what a waste of such gifts and talents that could have been used for God!

How about you? Are you wasting your life involved in things you have no business doing? If you are, listen to the haunting words of old from someone who "never said no to himself" and did all the crazy and inappropriate things he wanted to.

Solomon went 360 degrees and came full circle, ending back at the feet of God—totally submitted and obedient to the supremacy and power of God. Initially Solomon was broken, but then God restored him.

The beauty of where you are in your life is that you don't have to be broken! You can bypass a life of sin, bad habits, guilt, shame addictions, broken relationships, and all the other garbage that comes with trying to live a life without God.

Today you have the opportunity to begin the process to make things right in your life so you can spend your time knowing Jesus, loving Jesus, and living Jesus. Which will you choose today? I hope you'll choose Jesus!

Solomon's fourth conclusion goes hand in hand with his third. In fact, it's so related that it's the second half of the same verse. Solomon says that if you fear God—that is, respect Him and take Him seriously—then you'll naturally obey Him. Look again at the second part of verse 13 of Ecclesiastes 12: "obey God!" Did you notice that there's an exclamation point after that statement? I didn't put it there—Solomon did.

You can say you respect and love God all day long, but the bottom line is this: Is it evidenced by your words and actions? Are you obedient to God? Do you do what He asks you to do? Are you following the Ten Commandments? The NIV translates the second part of this verse "keep his commandments." If you respect and love somebody but don't do what they ask you to do, then how much do you really love them and are really obeying them? The Ten Commandments are all about relationships.

They're not suggestions. Are you listening to His voice when God speaks to you and convicts you of something that you shouldn't be doing? Or do you just ignore Him because you think you know best or don't care? If you're not obedient to Him now, you'll end up paying for it in the end. It's your decision. If you want to read something interesting, read the New Testament book of 1 John. You'll see the inseparable connection between love and obedience.

Solomon's last conclusion is the one that shuts everybody up! Christians and non-Christians alike seem to get *really* quiet and somber when you bring this topic up. Let's take a look at what Solomon had to say: "God will judge everything we do, even what is done in secret, whether good or bad" (Ecclesiastes 12:14). And that's the end of the book!

Isn't that crazy? What's the point Solomon is trying to make by ending the book so abruptly? Just this: Everything you do, everything you think, everything you say will one day be looked at by God. He will make a decision, and that decision will be *final.* Based upon what God decides, you'll spend eternity either with Him in heaven and the new earth or apart from Him burned up in the lake of fire (aka hell). There's no way to get around it!

At this point, if you haven't accepted Jesus Christ as your Lord and Savior and His death as a substitution for yours, please *do it now!* Don't wait another second! You have to understand something very important: hell was never meant for you or me. It was meant only for the devil and his demons (the angels that were thrown out of heaven after war broke out). Neither God nor I want you to burn in hell and be lost forever!

The topic of God's judgment is a really important and popular one these days with all that's happening around the world. I'm no Bible scholar and I'm not going to give you a class in the different beliefs and theories surrounding God's judgment, because in my eyes, it's real simple. Either you are for God, or you are against Him. There's no riding the fence here. If you're not 100 percent with God, then you're 100 percent against Him.

You see, God says in the Bible that if you're "friendly" with the world, then you're God's enemy! What does it mean to be friendly with the world? Well, it simply means to care more about what's happening in the world and what others think than what's happening with God and what He thinks. The word "enemy" is a strong word, and being called God's enemy makes me feel *really* uncomfortable. To tell you the truth, I don't even like writing those words.

But God wants you to make a decision, and you've got to make a decision—and make one today. Every day that you don't seriously think about this issue and make a conscious and clear decision for God, you've already made a decision for the devil. That's right—when you don't choose God, you automatically choose the devil's team. Yikes!

Some people say, "Oh, come on, I want to wait and see when things really start getting serious—then I'll clean up my life!"

Well, let me tell you what my father used to always say: "If you know better, do better!"

If it sounds as though I'm coming down hard on you, it's because I care about you, and I'm only reflecting what God is saying to you. This is a really important topic. The Bible describes the judgment in a bunch of different places in both the old and new testaments. It speaks about the "great white throne judgment" (Revelation 20:11-15) and the general judgment of the dead (Matthew 25:31-46).

So now that you know about Solomon's conclusions, what will you do with this information?

God created us to be perfect—to have a perfect relationship with Him. However, because of sin we've lost our perfection and therefore our relationship. With that sin comes a deep identity crisis. We each have a deep longing to identify with someone or something . . . to find where we fit in the "big picture."

We each have a hole in our soul, and so we fill our lives with stuff, desperately but uselessly trying to fill that hole—searching, like Solomon, with a hole that can be filled only by and with Jesus. We can find our full identity and meaning only through Him. Nothing else on this earth will do it. Pleasures and relationships won't do it. Knowledge and wisdom won't do it. Work and position won't do it. And money and wealth certainly won't do it.

It's my prayer that you'll make a decision for God and not for the devil! Remember, God's way is always the best way. Life is full of decisions, so make yours good ones. Make God first above all in your life, and you can't go wrong.